Charles Meynell, Henry Ignatius Dudley Ryder

Sermons for the spring quarter

Charles Meynell, Henry Ignatius Dudley Ryder

Sermons for the spring quarter

ISBN/EAN: 9783741194207

Manufactured in Europe, USA, Canada, Australia, Japa

Cover: Foto ©Lupo / pixelio.de

Manufactured and distributed by brebook publishing software (www.brebook.com)

Charles Meynell, Henry Ignatius Dudley Ryder

Sermons for the spring quarter

SERMONS.

SERMONS

FOR

THE SPRING QUARTER.

BY THE LATE
VERY REV. CHARLES MEYNELL, D.D.

EDITED BY

H. I. D. RYDER,
OF THE ORATORY.

FR. PUSTET,
PRINTER TO THE HOLY SEE AND THE S. CONGREGATION OF RITES.

FR. PUSTET & CO.,
NEW YORK AND CINCINNATI.
1883.

TO

SIR J. PERCIVAL AND LADY RADCLIFFE,

THESE LAST WORDS OF A DEAR FRIEND

ARE,

AT THAT FRIEND'S EXPRESS DESIRE,

AND AS A PLEDGE THAT HE WILL EVER HOLD THEM

IN HIS REMEMBRANCE,

RESPECTFULLY DEDICATED

BY THEIR OBEDIENT SERVANT,

THE EDITOR.

INTRODUCTORY MEMOIR.

—o—

THE duty of editing these Sermons was bequeathed to me by my dear friend Charles Meynell. He had himself almost prepared them for publication when he was attacked by a cruel disease, the hopeless nature of which at once declared itself. He lost no time in putting the Sermons into my hands, whilst expressing his regret that he had been unable to add two more, which would have completed his group on the Passion, and desiring me to dedicate them for him to the friends whose names stand at the head of this volume.

Dr. Meynell had in 1866 published a volume of "Short Sermons on Doctrinal Subjects," which went through two editions, and was much read, and used in the pulpit, both by Catholics and by those outside the Church. The characteristic of his Sermons, I venture to think, is the union of very careful elaboration, sometimes resulting in ornament, with great simplicity and directness of scope. From the choice of subject and manner of presenting it, his sermon was always to his audience an instruction in the art of religious thinking, and yet it appealed, though for the most part very quietly, to the affections. I doubt if his sermons, though always scholarly, ever went over the heads of his audience, although this was often made up of boys and illiterate persons. His preaching was always interesting to every one who heard him, gentle and simple, for this amongst other reasons, that he was himself so interested: he had ever something to show you that you must see; ever some tale to tell to which you must perforce listen.

Besides his sacred studies, his favourite reading was metaphysics—of which he was for many years Professor at Oscott College—poetry, and natural history. Essays on metaphysical and literary subjects were at intervals published by him, which many of his friends regarded as preludes to some important work. Perhaps, however, he was a man too various in his literary sympathies for the concentration necessary for any special protracted literary work.

He had as little as may be of the schoolmaster in his composition; yet no man had more exquisitely the gift of teaching boys to think, and to take an intelligent interest in their thoughts.

The last of his published work was his share in the Correspondence, "Proteus and Amadeus," edited by Mr. de Vere in 1878, in which Dr. Meynell sustains the part of Amadeus, the assertor and defender of the God of natural reason in the face of modern infidel objections. As Amadeus he appears as a shrewd and yet most genial disputant, and as a close observer and tender admirer of the animal creation. He had achieved, as he tells us, and as I can bear witness, that all but impossible task, according to Mr. Darwin, the complete domestication of the wild grey rabbit. No bad symbol this of many a feat accomplished amongst human fauna as untamable, but who were at a loss to resist the shy earnestness of our friend's manner.

The literary work he has left behind him, with all its excellence, is indeed but a small portion of the man, and of his work; for the work is the man. He attracted every one who came across him without effort,—without making himself in the least unlike himself,—through what was best in them. Sixth-form boys and little factory children were amongst his special favourites, and these perhaps loved him best: but I found that on the little bit of railway he was continually traversing, professional and commercial men going to their business of a morning would always ask the stationmaster, "Is the Doctor in the train?"—so that if possible they might get a five or ten minutes in his company. Indeed, although a certain shy gentleness formed part of his character, he was quite endlessly amusing.

He was educated at Oscott and the English College at Rome. He died after a long and painful illness of several months,—during which he exemplified the lesson of cheerful patience he had so assiduously taught,—on May 4, 1882, in the 54th year of his age, at his little mission of Caverswall, North Staffordshire, amid the obstinate hopes of his friends that he would yet be spared them.

To all who were in the habit of meeting him his death has marked the passage of something very pleasant and refreshing out of their lives. For myself, these lines, which are neither mine nor of him, may best express my feeling:—

> "What thoughtful friendship on thy deathbed died!
> Friend of my youth! whilst thou wert by my side
> Autumnal days still breathed a vernal breath;
> How like a charm thy life to me supplied
> All waste and injury of time or tide—
> How like a disenchantment was thy death."[1]

H. I. D. RYDER.

[1] Sir H. Taylor.

CONTENTS.

SERMON	PAGE
I. Predestination,	1
II. Judas,	14
III. Jacob's Wrestling and Job's Disputation,	29
IV. The Fall of Peter,	47
V. The Face of God,	62
VI. The Call of Pilate,	75
VII. The Penitent Thief,	89
VIII. The Temptation of the Cross,	99
IX. Our Blessed Saviour's Resurrection,	115
X. The Resurrection of the Body,	127
XI. The Penitential Spirit,	138
XII. The Bread of Life,	149
XIII. Time and Eternity,	160
XIV. Neither Cold nor Hot,	170
XV. Speculative Piety,	183
XVI. The Glory of God,	197
XVII. The Visible and Sacramental Advent,	212
XVIII. The Gift of the Holy Spirit,	225

I.

PREDESTINATION.

"For whom He foreknew, He also predestinated to be made conformable to the image of His Son; that He might be the firstborn amongst many brethren. And whom He predestinated, them He also called; and whom He called, them He also justified; and whom He justified, them He also glorified. What shall we say to these things? If God be for us, who is against us?"—ROM. viii. 29, 30, 31.

IT is not a little remarkable that these words of hope and encouragement should have been distorted into one of the gloomiest forms of heresy. But this is ever the way: the activity of perverse minds will be sure to corrupt and change into poison even their spiritual meat and drink; and, as the adage says, "Corruptio optimi pessima."[1] The Apostle had in view, in writing these lines, as we may gather from their context, the perilous circumstances of the Church at the time in which he wrote. The opposition of the world, the tribunal, chains, death— these, or the imminent risk of these, was the chosen portion of every Christian; but what then? What

[1] The corruption of the best is the worst corruption.

was man against God? They had not first elected themselves to be Christians: God had elected them. He had foreknown who would co-operate with His grace, to be made conformable, in these crosses, to the image of His divine Son; and whom He had foreknown, them He had elected, them called, them justified, that when their time was fulfilled, they might also be glorified. This was God's plan, and be sure He would carry it, no matter by what means, but He *would* carry it out.

Let them not fear then, but trust in God. "All things work together unto good for such as, according to His purpose, are called to be saints."[1] What could avail the counsels of men against the plan and purpose of God? What matter what tribunal condemned them, if He justified them? Yea, what matter though the world did the worst the world could do—though they suffered, died for the faith, if all the sufferings of this life "are not worthy to be compared with the glory to come, that shall be revealed in us?"[2] Such is the argument into the construction of which enter the words of the text, and which finishes with a torrent of fervid eloquence: "I am sure that neither death, nor life, nor angels, nor principalities, nor powers, nor things present, nor things to come, nor might, nor height, nor depth, nor any other creature shall be able to separate us from the love of God, which is in Christ Jesus our Lord."[3]

[1] Rom. viii. 28.   [2] Ibid. viii. 13.
[3] Ibid. viii. 38, 39.

Strange, I say, that words like these, which are plainly rather of a practical than doctrinal import, should have been construed as teaching a system of fatalism! Because men cannot, strictly speaking, thwart the purpose of God, therefore they have not free-will! Because grace and justification are from Him, therefore there is neither co-operation, nor the merit of co-operation in ourselves! Or, because it suits the Apostle's purpose to treat in this place of God's part in the affair of salvation, therefore all other passages of Holy Scripture are to be set aside, or explained away, which just as distinctly enunciate the doctrines of free-will and the merit of good works! But enough on this head; for I well understand that a merely controversial treatment of the subject would be unsuitable in the present circumstances. I intend rather to answer a question which is sometimes asked by those who are striving to lead spiritual lives, and are habituated to religious thought, viz., whether the Church of God does not both use the word, and teach, in some sense or other, the doctrine of Predestination, and whether it be not a very awful and embarrassing subject?

I answer that the word certainly occurs in Holy Scripture, as instanced in the text. It is also used in the liturgy of the Church, as we are reminded by the remarkable "secret prayer," which is read in the Mass during this season,[1] and which petitions that the Book of Predestination may retain the names of

---

[1] "Ut omnium fidelium nomina beatæ Predestinationis Liber adscripta retineat." Secret prayer, read in the Mass on Ash-Wednesday.

all the faithful inscribed therein. And this use of the word makes it pertinent to speak upon the subject at this time, when the Church herself reminds us of it.

Now the very fact that the Church uses the word implies that she teaches the doctrine of Predestination, viz., that God has, beforehand, elected to everlasting life such as He foreknew would be His by co-operation with grace in order to good works; but I need hardly say, that any such sense of the word as would go to deny that salvation is also the result of co-operation and the reward of good works, is neither the meaning of the Church, nor allowed to be held or taught in the Church. And as to whether the subject be not awful and embarrassing, this, because it is of practical importance, I wish to handle.

Now that the point may be very embarrassing to the reason, in the case of some persons, may be granted; though others cannot see here a difficulty of the reason; so far at least as regards the reconciliation of Predestination and free-will. That the doctrine of Predestination is a mystery, they do not indeed deny; for the Church teaches that it is. The whole subject of grace is full of mystery; but it is not in the reconciliation of Predestination with free-will, they say, that the mystery consists. That God foresees that such or such persons will comply with His grace, and that they are consequently pre-elected to everlasting life, is a fact, they argue, which no more controls the free-will of such persons, than if, suppose, we could foresee it ourselves. But men's minds are differently constituted, and that is sometimes a difficulty to one, which seems as clear as noon-day to another. For the sake of such persons, then, who acknowledge a difficulty of the reason here, I trust to show that, if there is indeed a difficulty, this is not of the slightest practical importance; and that, if they are embarrassed by it, or affrighted at it, or if, as I believe is the case with some persons, they take a kind of gloomy pleasure in bewildering themselves about it, this is owing either to ignorance, or to a certain secret pride, or to a morbid, unhealthy frame of mind, the fancies of which it is very foolish to encourage, or to all these causes combined. And this being the case, it seems better to treat the subject as a mother, or nurse, is wont to treat some bugbear that affrights the fancy of a child; for she brings the suspected object into the full light, and makes the child see plainly what manner of thing it is that caused its terror, and that the object is good and harmless as it really is. This method, then, I will adopt on the present occasion.

Now, they who maintain that the reconciliation of Predestination with free-will is a difficulty of the reason, or rather that it is more than a mere difficulty of the reason—that it is one of those hidden things which it is not given to the mind of man to comprehend, will probably state their case somewhat as follows:—

They will say that man has certainly free-will, for this is a fact that is witnessed by each man's own conscience; because the very reproach of conscience imports that we deliberately chose evil where we might have chosen good. Man is free then. But while the conscience witnesses that man is free, revelation also witnesses that it is not in man's power to frustrate the designs of God; that He moves, superintends, controls, directs the universal Scheme of Things; and that nothing happens without His permission, or else He would not be sovereign Lord and Master in His own creation. But how, it is asked, can we reconcile the sovereign dominion of the Creator with the free-will of the creature? How can God do as He wills with the creature, while the creature is also free to do as he wills with himself? They maintain that we cannot effect this reconciliation; that the matter lies beyond the domain of reason; that it is a matter, not for the exercise of reason, but for the exercise of faith; that we must believe both the voice of God which speaks to us in revelation, and the voice of God which speaks to us in conscience; without perplexing ourselves as to how the two statements are reconcilable, since both are equally the voice of God, who can neither deceive nor be deceived; that we hold in our hands, as it were, the two ends of a chain which reaches into the Infinite; but where they meet we cannot tell, until we see the face of God.

Now I will not inquire whether or not this be a correct statement of the case, or whether or not a satisfactory answer to the difficulty can be given; for I will not appear so vain as to attach any importance to what I might think on a matter upon which the greatest and holiest of thinkers have differed. I will only suppose, for argument's sake, that the difficulty is nowise to be solved by human ingenuity. Yet you will have observed, brethren, that the knot of the difficulty (granting that there is one) resides, not in a matter that we are conversant with, but in a matter about which we know little or nothing. I mean that, when we reason *upwards*, from ourselves to the incomprehensible Creator, we do not meet the difficulty at all.

Thus we are conscious of a law within ourselves, which directs us as to right and wrong; but the very fact that we are so conscious, as we have seen already, implies freedom; there being no room for either praise or blame where there is compulsion. Now the fact of a moral law within us implies the fact of a Lawgiver, who has set this law in our hearts, and who, like the law itself, is moral and holy; who, that is to say, will judge us, and reward, or punish, according to the quality of our works, as good or evil. But God could not judge us morally, or righteously, in the case that He either exercised or allowed to be exercised on us any influence which should compel the will, since such compulsion once more would destroy the morality of our deeds.

Reasoning, then, in this manner, from our own side in creation to that of God, I say, the difficulty does not occur. It is only in reasoning *downwards*, from the notion of God as Prime Mover and Director of the universal Scheme of Things, that the difficulty occurs as to how His influence can be consistent with human liberty. And really what does the knowledge of such worms of the earth as we are amount to, on the influence which God exerts as Prime Mover, either in the order of nature, or that of grace? Or what have the greatest intellects that ever flourished — what have they ever taught, or known, about the universal Scheme of Things? And if a mere speculation of this nature has led some into heresy, or so wrought upon others as to drive them distracted, I can only repeat what I have said, that ignorance, or pride, or a morbid frame of mind must be assigned as the account of such extravagancies.

Nor ought a well-balanced mind, and one that is thoroughly broken in to the thought of God, to be much surprised at any apparent contradiction of the reason which may arise out of the consideration of religious matters, since it is clear that there can be no real contradiction. And if there appear to be such, this is not owing to the reason itself, but to the obscurity of the matters on which the reasoning powers are exercised. An apparent clash of the reason with itself is not unusual, even when science is engaged with the investigation of God's visible creations. Thus, at one time, from the very same fact, that the moon presented always the same face to the earth, it was equally argued, on one side and on the other, both that she did and did not revolve around her own centre.[1] And what is very remarkable, men of

[1] "Il arrive souvent [à la raison humaine] de se contredire elle-même, suivant qu'elle considère son objet sous deux points de vue différents. M. de Mairan a jugé la dispute de deux célèbres astronomes, dispute qui était résultée d'une semblable difficulté sur le choix d'un point de

science judged that the reasoning of the disputants on either side was equally sound and legitimate; and therefore the contradiction was certainly not owing to the reason: it was, in reality, owing to the fact that either arguer differed from the other as to the point of view selected for observation; and each of them had argued rightly from his own point of view. As to which was the best point of view, this was a question which would be decided by further experience; and so the difficulty would vanish.

But observe that, in applying this case to illustrate the matter in hand, there is, in this life at least, no enlarged experience, no experience whatsoever, to correct the reasonings of men upon the things of God. Ever hard and difficult must remain those things which are hard and difficult, until, instead of this twilight of the reason, shall come the fulness of the brightness of His day, and "in His Light, we shall see light."[1] Yet, while it is given us only to believe, without seeing; while we may reason about divine things, and perhaps, reasoning from opposite points of view, arrive at conflicting conclusions, this is one plain point of practical wisdom, that it is certainly safer, to say the least, to argue from the point

---

vue, comme un phénomène assez digne de remarque pour faire à ce sujet une dissertation particulière. L'un raisonnait ainsi : *La lune tourne autour de son axe*, parce qu'elle montre constamment le même côté à la terre ; l'autre ainsi : *La lune ne tourne pas autour de son axe*, précisément parce qu'elle montre toujours le même côté à la terre. Les deux raisonnements étaient vrais, suivant le point de vue d'où l'on voulait observer le mouvement de la lune." Kant. *Critique de la raison pure.* Tom. ii. p. 161.

[1] Ps. xxxv. 10.

of view where we know something, than from that where we know little or nothing. I wish, observe, always to treat the subject practically; and it is a matter of practical experience that man has free-will; while, on the other hand, that the Scheme of Things, as mere worms like ourselves may conceive of it, seems, if it does seem, inconsistent with this fact, is a mere speculation, which, whatever advantages it may possess as a speculation, is of no practical importance whatsoever. Granting that it is true, yet, for want of some other truth which we do not know (and which might possibly, after all, reconcile it with free-will), it is to us practically as if it were false. And whatever else be said of it, it would certainly be the grossest folly to act upon it, or, in any degree, to allow it to influence our minds for evil.

Having thus, I trust, divested the subject of its fancied terrors, let us now, my brethren, consider the subject of Predestination as the Apostle considers it, and as a source, not of scruple and alarm, but of hope and loving confidence in God. Our salvation, as you well know, does not, in one sense, depend upon ourselves; and it is well that it does not. For, if salvation depended merely upon ourselves, it is to be feared that many would be lost through presumption. They would think that they might trifle on, and tamper with the powers of evil, or they would actually pursue a course of sinning, thinking they might safely do so, as long as it pleased them, since they always had the remedy in their own hands, and it would be quite time enough to turn to God when they were well wearied of the world ; and, meantime, they would have put on the second nature of evil habit, and, in spite of grace, they would ever find it too great a wrench to part with themselves and their passions.

But others, instead, would surely fall into downright despair. For what man that rightly considers himself, and what he is by nature—how changeful and inconstant, how inflamed by passion, how beset with snares and temptations from without, how doubtful and treacherous within, how fearfully prone to evil, how dull and sluggish to good, how easily entangled by habit, how feeble to break its meshes asunder, how easily elated, how suddenly depressed—who, I say, that considers these things, will not thank God a thousand times that he is not wholly in his own keeping? But since salvation lies thus beyond your own natural powers, as it certainly does, this is God's eternal decree and purpose, this, brethren, is your Predestination, that He will save you, if only you, on your part, will be saved. He will enlighten, guide, and strengthen you to the last, if only you will still and ever cleave to Him, and co-operate heart and soul with Him. He predestinated them "whom He foreknew" would "be made conformable to the image of His Son." How simple! He has beforehand chosen you, if you have since chosen Him; He has called, if you have hearkened ; He has justified, if you love Him with all your heart; He will glorify, if you will be "faithful unto death." "What shall we say to these things? If God be for us, who is against us?" What can thwart or turn Him? What can make *His* plan miscarry? In His strong keeping, beneath the shelter of His wings, you shall walk in safety through sunshine and shade, even to the Holy Mountain of God. What can temptation, or troubles, or pains, or losses, or the power and craft of men, or the subtleties of demons, or the agonies of death avail against Him? He will make all things work together for your good; He will stay you up when you faint; He will strengthen the trembling knees; He will dash aside all the fiery darts of the Evil One; He will, at length, lay all your enemies at your feet; He will confirm and establish you for ever.

But should you answer: "Alas! it is not God, it is myself that I distrust. The end is not yet: would only that I knew I should persevere to the end! But when I think how many better than myself have turned aside—then indeed I fear and tremble for myself."—Oh, happy fear and trembling, then! Oh, sure and certain sign of Predestination, if only it lead you all the more to lean on God, and ever the more to beg His help! There was one you may sometimes have read of, who, all anxious and wavering between hope and fear, threw himself on the pavement of the church, and thus prayed before the altar: "Oh, if I only knew that I should persevere!" when, on the instant, he heard within himself this answer: "And if thou didst know this, what wouldst thou do? Do now what thou wouldst then do, and thou shalt be perfectly secure."[1]

[1] Imitation of Christ, book i. chap. 25.

II.

JUDAS.

"His own iniquities catch the wicked man; and he is fast bound with the ropes of his own sins."—PROV. v. 22.

TO an upright honest man, a criminal such as Judas Iscariot, who betrayed our Blessed Saviour, seems to be a very mystery of iniquity; but so, to a certain extent, does any criminal at all. The miser, the drunkard, the thief, the murderer, are only understood by us in the proportion that we feel within our breasts certain seeds of a kindred evil, which other circumstances might foster into kindred crime. Certainly the journals of the day sometimes startle us by revealing crimes so abominable and inhuman, so gross and foul in their conception, so ghastly and hideous in their execution, that nothing seems equal to account for them, save either the agency of the devil, or downright madness. But the devil, subtle and powerful as he is, has no power over the soul, except such as we ourselves allow him. He may enter into the house and make there the abomination of desolation; but not until the keeper of the house has himself unbolted and unbarred to him, and handed over the keys of all its stores and treasures. And as to madness: well, there is certainly a great deal of truth in this account of the matter. For a vicious habit, once contracted and become inveterate (no matter what kind the habit may be), does become at length a kind of mania. It so binds, drives, blinds, enslaves, and unmans its unhappy victim, that, as to all those matters in which his ruling passion is affected, he can scarcely bring himself to act like a rational creature. Then indeed the man becomes a fitting agent for the schemes of the Evil One; and there is no suggestion so foul but he will listen to it; no act so unseemly, gross, and hideous, but he will lend himself to its execution. He is deaf to reasoning; he is out of the reach of persuasion; he knows no bounds of moderation. Duty, conscience, self-respect, human respect, worldly prudence—all are cast to the winds. And in this depth of depravity, there is only the lower deep of despair to complete his ruin.

There is, in short, no mystery of iniquity in the enormous excesses of the ruling passion; and if we wonder at them, this is only because we do not realise the *force of habit;* just as, for a like reason, we wonder to see how the ivy growth has burst a stone wall asunder, or when, in balancing our accounts, we discover how quickly certain paltry matters have swollen into a considerable sum. This only consideration, of the force of habit in the ruling passion, seems sufficient of itself to account for a Judas or any other criminal. And in its light I will endeavour, out of the scattered notices of him furnished in the Holy Gospels, to build up his character, such as I conceive it to have been, and to trace his career for our instruction.

At what period in the life of Judas it was that he began that gradual career of evil, which ended at last in unspeakable wickedness, we are not told: the gospel only presents to us the result. But we must believe that it *was* gradual; for no man becomes depraved on a sudden. Is it possible that the two or three short years of our Blessed Saviour's public ministry should suffice to account for this enormous growth of villany? that the man should have changed from saint, almost, to criminal, with such incredible swiftness? Well, if it be written of the just man that, "in a short space he fulfilled a long time," why may not this also be the case with the wicked? But on the other hand, St. John says plainly that the man was a thief, and I venture to say that, as a rule, habits of theft and deceitfulness are acquired in childhood, or not at all. That my trusty friend should betray me, or turn thief, I should think a thing impossible, as that the rivers should run backwards!

But at what period soever it was that Judas first started on his downward course, it is enough for our present purpose that, when our Blessed Lord first chose, and numbered him amongst the twelve Apostles, he was either a saint, or on the road to saintliness. He was one of the first disciples of Christ, who witnessed His great miracles, who hung on His lips when He preached, who believed in Him as the promised Saviour, who forsook all things to follow Him, and was chosen by Him to the sacred ministry. If his former career had been corrupt and sinful, as it probably was, yet, in the sweet light of his Saviour's countenance, he had learnt to detest and alter his old crooked ways. He was as earnest and sincere, it is likely, as was Zaccheus himself, who was also a convert from dishonest practices. But surely the very fact that our Blessed Saviour called him to the Apostolate is proof enough of his sincerity at the time. And by the same token, he would have had those other qualities which are considered the marks of such a vocation—a certain savour of heavenly things, a zeal for God's honour and the salvation of souls, a relish for ministerial duty; and, most distinctly, the sweet gift of sympathy and human kindness; else, surely, he had never been called at all to the Priesthood.

No doubt, as a matter of fancy, it would be more agreeable to conceive Judas as being devoid of amiable qualities; but the fancy is only childish. There are no *bad men*, except those who have made themselves such. It is the eternal disgrace of Satan himself, not that he is devil, but that he is fallen angel; and that he himself is the author of this unsightly ruin. And so likewise as to Judas, what is hateful in him, and what points the moral of his story is, not that he was villain by nature, but that he marred and ruined in himself the makings of a saint.

The other eleven Apostles, one would think, must have known something of their comrade's antecedents; for the early scenes of our Lord's labours in the ministry were not large towns or cities, but little villages, where everybody knew everybody. But it would little matter to them what the man *had been*. Jesus came to save sinners like Judas. The office of steward, to which he was appointed, showed their perfect confidence in him; perhaps was allotted to him for that very purpose. Anyhow, they availed themselves of his tact for management; and Judas kept the purse, and, I suppose, acquitted himself generally as steward and caterer for the little flock. But their habits were plain and simple, and their wants such as the commonest fare would satisfy, so that the office of steward would hardly interfere with the work of the ministry, which Judas would have to discharge like the rest. "Go and preach," said their Divine Master, "saying, 'The kingdom of heaven is at hand.' Heal the sick; raise the dead; cleanse the lepers; cast out devils. Freely have ye received, freely give."[1] In such gracious works of mercy and charity was Judas to have sanctified and schooled himself for the sacred office of the Priesthood; with what disastrous result we know.

When, then, did the wily serpent begin, first to fascinate, and then to wind coil after coil about his victim, till the Christ in his heart was dead, the new man unmade, and the old, unsavoury Judas revived? We do not know. He could not, most

[1] Matt. x. 7, 8.

likely, have said himself (so gradual are the approaches of evil) when the mischief actually began in him. No matter: his fall, we may well believe, was like another fall. The safeguards of virtue would go first. He broke his rule, and had a purse of his own — perhaps telling himself, that the rule against private money did not bind him as the manager. If he sometimes used the common fund for his own private purposes, he could easily make that good, on occasion. But then, when he remembered that he had failed to do so, he might think, After all, did it matter? If the disciples had wherewith to meet the demands of each day as it came round, what more did they want? Had they not been told, that it was a heathen thought to care overmuch about money? Then, when it became clear as noonday, even to himself, that he was simply pilfering, the old habit was grown now too strong, and fairly overmastered him; and so, in the words of the text, "he is fast bound with the ropes of his own sins."

He has now a line to pass over, which every sinner must pass over in order to become reprobate —the line, I mean, which divides between the sin of *frailty* and the sin of *malice*. At first he sins against the promptings of his better nature, and, as it were, in spite of himself. He has taken the wrong road; but he does not intend to walk in it unto the end. Sooner or later, however, he sees that he must make his choice. Amendment becomes every day more and more difficult, and will shortly become, humanly speaking, impossible. If the thing is to be done at all, it must be done at once—or never. He has his way to choose—and he chooses it.

But before it came to this point, be sure that, even while he had contrived to disguise his dirty vice to himself, others were not quite unaware of the mischief that was hatching in him; for "the attire of the body, and the laughter of the teeth, and the gait of the man show what he is."[1] The hollow look, the obsequious shrug, the unctuous smile, the over-acted surprise, when something loose in his accounts, or his account of his accounts, has been detected, show plainly that the man has something to hide. And this necessity of hiding leads him at last to set the crown on his deceit by cloaking malice with the guilt of hypocrisy. And so, when Mary Magdalen sheds the precious spikenard upon the sacred feet of our Blessed Saviour, in the house of Simon the leper, this man lifts up hands and eyes of astonishment, and clucks the mouth with vexation; and, "To what purpose," he exclaims, "is this waste? Why was not this ointment sold for three hundred pence, and given to the poor?"[2] "But this he said," St. John remarks, "not because he cared for the poor, but because he was a thief, and having the purse, carried the matters that were put therein."[3]

But, to what end were these his petty thefts? What was he hoarding for? What did he mean to

---

[1] Ecclus. xix. 27. [2] Matt. xxvi. 8. John xii. 5.
[3] Ibid. xii. 6.

do with the money, when the hoard was made up? He had not those vices which are costly in the gratification, else it is strange that nothing of the kind is suggested in the Gospel. He had not, or at least he need not have had, any scheme at all as to the purpose of the money. In short, there needs not to be given any account of his vice, for the simple reason that it is unaccountable; and that is what we mean by saying of such a vice that it is a *mania*.

But it may be asked, had he lost the Faith? Could this man have really believed in his heart *Who* Jesus was, who stood daily in their midst, and yet sin as he sinned? This question I will answer by another: Do Christians nowadays believe, *when they sin*, in spite of the awful, though hidden Presence, before whose face we sometimes kneel? If so, then Judas also, we may suppose, believed. Faith is the eye of the soul, which the ruling passion need not blind; but then how it darkens! A cloud, gross and palpable, thickens before the face of God and the eternal, saving, truths. And now the abode is made ready for the Prince of Darkness; and "Satan entered into Judas."[1] And so, while the priests are scheming together, in the house of Caiphas, how they might "by subtlety apprehend Jesus," behold into their midst steals the very man for their purpose; and with a cunning light in his eye, chuckles forth: "What will you give me, and I will deliver Him unto you? And

[1] Luke xxii. 3.

they appointed him thirty pieces of silver"[1]—about three pounds and sixteen shillings of our money!

A sudden change this would seem, from the sneaking, timorous pilferer, to the brow-hardened villain! Still, I cannot think the manner of his fall different from that of another fall. The downward pace ever multiplies itself in velocity; and the climax of villany always astonishes those who have not, like the criminal himself, had experience of the several grades in the descent. Then we must bear in mind the blinding power of sin. No doubt, Judas had told himself: If this man be the Son of God, no harm is done: He will escape out of their hands by miracle, as He has escaped before. The sequel shows, at any rate, that the result of his crime—the death of Jesus, this was what he neither intended nor expected.

But account for it as we may, oh, he is changed indeed! How lightly, how gaily now, almost, he wears his cloak of hypocrisy! The impudent effrontery of his bearing at the Last Supper has an air about it almost of innocence. Words of warning are being uttered by the Divine Master; and he whom they concern knows well enough at whom the warning is pointed. But the devil within him sustains, and he quails not at voice or sign. "Amen, I say unto you, that one of you is about to betray Me," and "The Son of Man indeed goeth, as it is written of Him: but woe to that man by whom the Son of Man shall be betrayed! It were better for him if that man had not been born."[2] And while a dark

---

[1] Matt. xxvi. 15.   [2] Ibid. xxvi. 21, 24.

shadow overspreads the faces of the disciples, as each one asks in dismay, "Is it I, Lord?" this man, too, at last opens his mouth; and since he dares to ask the question at all, asks it, no doubt, with bold front, and unfaltering accent. "He who dippeth his hand with Me into the dish," was the secret sign which Jesus gave to the Beloved Disciple,[1] "he shall betray Me." And Judas reached forth his hand: "Is it I, Rabbi?" he asks. "Thou hast said it," was the answer. "What thou dost, do quickly."[2] And so he vanished into the night; and quickly he did it, and thoroughly he acquitted himself, down to the signal kiss in the garden.

Mark well, brethren, the next phase in his career, for it is instructive. The devil, in order to drive him into despair, now changes in him into an angel of light. Hitherto he had walked as in a cloud; but no sooner had he heard from Pilate's lips the sentence of condemnation, than the glare as of noon-day breaks on his soul. He *repented himself*, we read, when he saw that Jesus was condemned, but his is a repentance that neither asks nor hopes for pardon.—What hast thou done? says the voice within him: A crime so foully black, so hugely hideous, that it wants a name. In what corner wilt thou hide thee away, oh! ever accursed of God and men?—Then the fancy strikes him that he will go back at once to the priests, return to them the blood-money, and be off from the bargain. A silly thought, now that the

---

[1] John xiii. 26. [2] Matt. xxvi. 25; John xiii. 27.

money had wrought the mischief for which he had it! but remorse drives him, and he can no longer brook the sight of those once coveted pieces. So to the priests he goes, and, "I have sinned," he moans, "in betraying innocent blood!" "What is that to us?" they scornfully answer; "look thou to it."[1] Then, in the frenzy of his despair, he hurls down the glittering coins on the pavement, and is gone. But whither, and to what end! Well may he pause and doubt, irresolute, before he goes to such a deed as blots out heaven and earth, and Jesus and mercy for evermore; embraces evil as the sovereign good; enthrones Satan for God; and is so much worse even than shedding the Blood of Christ, that it makes void the Blood which He has shed; an act mean and cowardly, as it is ghastly and inhuman. Make an end, says the Tempter; and he will make an end, he tells himself, as he strides off, with hurried step, to such a wild and lonely spot as the nature of the crime indicates. Quickly he goes, lest, even at the last moment, his heart fail him, and he repent him of his ungodly repentance. Wilfully he shuts his eyes to the sweet, pleading face of Jesus Christ, and wilfully he stops his ears to every angel voice that cries to him on his path, to have mercy on himself. He wants not salvation but destruction. He rushes on his ruin. He is mad, if you will; but it is the madness which has possessed him all along—the madness of sin. Then at length he halts, in some such lone, weird spot as best may hide the ignominy

[1] Matt. xxvii. 4.

of his passage; and there with fierce, hasty hand
adjusts the fatal halter. "And being hanged," we
read, "he burst asunder in the midst, and all his
bowels gushed out." And so he passed unto his
place.

Thus have I set before you, brethren, in the person
of Judas, the history of a ruling passion. Do not put
its lesson from you, as one with which you are not
concerned, which you are not likely to want. True
that the sin of theft is, to many persons, a sin almost
impossible; they could not even be tempted to commit it; they would loathe too, in their inmost hearts,
the path of treachery and miserly hoarding. Nevertheless, the story of Judas has its warning for all of
us. For each one of us has in him, by reason of his
sinful origin, some one or other ruling passion, which,
if unwatched, will become dangerous; if habitually
indulged, will be ruinous. Your way is not the way
of Judas, God forbid! but what then is your way?
What is it troubles, chiefly, your peace of soul?
What mostly crops up, when you examine your
conscience? What infests unbidden your waking
thoughts, your dreams by night? What most alarms
on the thought of death? Beware of *that*, whatever
it be. Stifle it, stamp it out, if you can; but never,
anyhow, never with it be truce of war; never allow
it the dominion over you, or it will change you. The
mischief will not end with itself; it will become a
brood. It will bring you at last the way you now
loathe. It will lead to sin as odious as the sin of
Judas, I do not say, merely because we cannot com-

pare one sinful passion with another. Whether is it worse that one manner of sinning likens a man unto a devil, or that another lowers him beneath the brute? Pride, lust, revenge, sloth, avarice, drunkenness, each has its own proper malice, and is sovereign in its own special deformity. But the rise, progress, and result of every evil passion is the same—begotten in selfishness, fostered by habit, and leading of its own nature to crime, to madness, and despair.

I do not merely mean the despair that goes to self-destruction. But oh, there is a despair that lives on! The man has chosen his way; and though he knows that his way leads to the gates of hell, yet he knows also that he will not depart from it. It is not that he loves his way; for, in his heart, he loathes it; but he does not even propose to alter it. He has simply given up the hope of ever doing any good. His bones are filled with the vices of his youth, and though there be balm in Gilead, he does not even wish to be healed. In vain for him the Lord's Day invites to worship, thanksgiving, and praise; in vain Jesus Christ is seated, in the person of His minister, in the judgment-seat of mercy; in vain His mystical bloodshedding in Holy Mass; in vain His solemn call in the ministry of the Word; in vain season of sweet festival or salutary fast, and all the loving contrivances of a God of love! That God would forgive even him he knows well; but he knows also that such forgiveness would involve the change of heart that he will not make; and he has the sense to see that a mock repentance would serve no purpose. Yea, he will die and give no sign, but pass, like the beasts that perish, to the abode of his eternity! How can God, all good and powerful as He is, save this man who will not have salvation?

And he is traitor too. A son of God, in Baptism, and heir of heaven; by free choice a child of hell, and slave of Satan. A soldier of Jesus Christ, in Confirmation; but, by the same token, a coward deserter, employed in the devil's pay and service. And is it not a traitor's act to have ruined in himself the temple of the Holy Ghost? to have defiled the Sacraments? to have dragged the name of Christ in the mire? But oh, brethren, be sure that God will forgive us every sin but our despair which refuses to be forgiven. This is the sin of sins; because it insults His love—the dearest of all His attributes, and makes void the Blood which He has shed. Many and great though our iniquities, yet far more abundant are His mercies. We may have woven fast about us the cords of sin, but He will break our bonds asunder. We may have put on the second nature of evil habit; but He will make us to be a new creature in Jesus Christ. He will work for us miracles of grace, if only we will seek Him with all our mind and heart. Sin-stained as we are He will take us back unto His bosom; He will make His lamp to shine again over our head; He will make Himself sweet in our breasts as in the days gone by, before the heavens and earth were darkened in our sin.

And oh, my young friends, whose way is still to choose, who happily have never known the fierce bondage of sin; know that also Judas was once such as you; and that you, save by God's grace, may become such as he! It is a fearful thought which ought to sober you. Beware the beginnings: set not so much as a foot in the path which he trod. Be sure that all is not well with you, if you dare not look your friends straight in the face. Cast out the poison in the Sacrament of Penance, or it will destroy you; it will blind your soul; it will harden your heart; it will darken to you the face of God. Strive earnestly to cultivate good habits while you are young, and they will strengthen with advancing years. But remember that to persevere is not given us of our own strength; and ask it heartily, and constantly of Him whose gift it is.

III.

JACOB'S WRESTLING AND JOB'S DISPUTATION.

"Thy knowledge is become wonderful to me: it is high, and I cannot reach it."—Ps. cxxxviii. 6.

THERE are two remarkable, not to say startling, events recorded in the Old Testament, which, in the likeness of their main features, are suggestive of one another, and seem to challenge comparison. I refer to Jacob's Wrestling and Job's Disputation with God. The facts in both cases are, I suppose, sufficiently familiar to you; I will therefore only touch upon the following points of contact in the narration of them:—

The angel who acted, or spoke, on either occasion, bore the name of God, and acted or spoke in the person of God. The strife was real, but it is hardly necessary to say, not hostile. Jacob, though overcome and disabled, still clave to his mysterious Antagonist, saying, "I will not let Thee go, unless Thou bless me."[1] It was Job's great grief which prompted his most impassioned laments, that God

---
[1] Gen. xxxii. 26.

appeared to him in the light of an Adversary; but, "Though He should slay me," he said, "I will trust in Him."¹ In both cases, while the Almighty confounds His human opponent, yet He shows Himself pleased with his bearing in the conflict. He frustrated Jacob's strength by touching a sinew of his thigh, but He gave him the blessing ere He departed. "Jacob asked Him, 'Tell me by what Name Thou art called.' He answered, 'Why dost thou ask My Name;' and He blessed him in the same place."² At first, He addresses Job in the language of stern rebuke: "Shall he that contendeth with God be so easily silenced? Surely he that reproveth God, ought to answer Him;"³ and yet, while He silenced him in the argument, God justified His servant before the friends, restored him to health, and re-endowed him with worldly substance and prosperity. I will only add that Jacob, as well as Job, knew, at least after the vision, that God had been his Opponent; for he said, "I have seen God face to face, and my soul has been saved."⁴

Now various comments have been made upon both these events, into the consideration of which I shall not enter, as I only propose to derive from them some general lesson for our instruction. Whatsoever construction be put upon them the facts remain, that Jacob wrestled with God, and Job disputed with Him. There was, at any rate, a contest of some kind or other between God and man; and

---

¹ Job xiii. 15.   ² Gen. xxxii. 29.
³ Job xxxix. 32.   ⁴ Gen. xxxii. 30.

what are we to think of it? Shall man dare, in whatsoever sense, to measure his strength with God; or ought he, if indeed he dare? Can he who ventures to strive with God, in word or deed, so much as know what he is doing? Can he really know who his Adversary is, or knowing, not tremble for the issue?

And here I cannot forbear remarking that it were well indeed if men kept this view of the matter steadily before their eyes; for what else does the sinner, in the act of sinning, but strive with God, but match himself against the Almighty, and dare Him to do His worst? He does not intend this, it is true; but whatever he intends, that is what he *does;* whatever he intends, that is the meaning of the act.

But this is not to my present purpose. I wish to show you, brethren, that, as there is an unlawful, so is there a lawful struggle and disputation with God —surely the instances in question are meant to teach us that there is—a conflict which is not one of hostility, but of friendship; and one in which God overthrows indeed, but only to raise us the higher; and in which, while He prevails against us, yet we also, in another sense, prevail against Him, and compel a blessing on our endeavours. But what kind of conflict? This is signified by the Patriarch's request, "Tell me by what Name Thou art called?" which in Hebrew phrase (because the Hebrew names have a graphic power) was equivalent to saying, "Tell me *what Thou art*"—as though, in short, he would inquire into the mystery of God's Being. Now, since the argument of the Book of Job, on the whole, is the mysteriousness of God's dealings with mankind, we see, putting these two things together, that the lesson of Jacob's Wrestling and of Job's Disputation with God is the same lesson, though with a different application. The former teaches that God is incomprehensible in Himself; the latter that He is incomprehensible in His works.

And now, my brethren, you see in what sense we may and must measure our strength with God. He is awfully, fearfully above us in the wondrous mystery of His Being; we feel that He is; but it is only in the endeavour to measure ourselves with Him that we are made to feel it. He is incomprehensible; but if we would fully learn the lesson, we must dare the attempt to comprehend Him. We must, with all reverence, search into His Majesty that we may be overwhelmed with His glory, and so come to the knowledge both of Him and of ourselves.

And who is there amongst us that has not experienced such a spiritual wrestling and disputation with God? Who is there amongst us so dull or unthinking, so devoid of natural curiosity, or so earthly and carnal that he has not, at some time or other, looked so directly and steadfastly in the face of that Mystery of Mysteries which we name God, that it has blinded or scared him? For it is with the thought of God as with the sight of the ocean. The first superficial glance at the sea, as it shoals upon the shore, refreshes the eyes, gladdens the spirits, and soothes and comforts the whole man; but who can look without awe upon the immeasurable waste of desert waters beyond? or who shall consider unmoved the terrific might that slumbers in its depths? The mind is held amazed and spell-bound by the overwhelming grandeur of its object, and its powers are paralysed. And so it is with that Almighty Being of which the ocean is the fittest symbol. The first shallow thought of God sustains and comforts the soul. It affords a standing-ground and a resting-place to the reason which is embarrassed by the problem of existence: it gives the mind a centre, and a point of view, and just the explanation of things which man requires in the first place as a rational being. There is wanting a reason for all things that exist; and God is that Reason. There is wanting a cause to account for all things else; but there must have been a First Cause, or else nothing would be accounted for; and this First Cause of all things is God. Moreover, this world which we inhabit bears upon it evident marks of design (just as much as a watch, or any other piece of mechanism); it was He who designed it. The whole universe is a vast system governed by laws; it was He that planned it; that gave it laws, that governs it. Thus, apart from revelation, to the existence of God we are led by the necessity of the case. There must be God or nothingness.

Here stay, here rest, and all is satisfactory and intelligible. But should you ask, "And why then God, and why not nothingness?"—ah! then comes the wrestle in which God strikes the soul to earth, trembling and confounded, scorched and dazzled by the white light which surrounds His throne: "Tell me by what Name Thou art called?" it is asked— Tell me, Dread Mystery, what Thou art? And a flash of blinding light is the answer: "Why dost thou ask My Name?" Yet fear not: He is not angry; but thus and ever must He prevail in the naked wonder of His Being, and bring into subjection every created intelligence.

And as with the Being itself, so with the attributes of God: on the surface all is light; within the depths all is awe and wonder. A rational account of the Deity seems, at first sight, possible, and is so indeed to a certain extent, else there could be no such science as theology. Given the mere notion of God as a self-existent Being, and reason proceeds, in the light of this idea, to establish His essential attributes. Since God exists, for the very reason that He exists, He has every real perfection—He is infinite in perfection: I mean that there is just the same reason for His being infinite as there is for His being at all; that He exists always, for the same reason that He exists at any time; that He is everywhere, for the same reason that He is anywhere. And so of His other attributes: because He is powerful, He is omnipotent; because He is wise, He is omniscient; because He is good, He is all-perfect. And all this is only saying that He is God. It is, in effect, one and the same thing to be uncreated and to be infinite; as it is, on the other hand, one and the same thing to be created and to be limited. And what reason declares of the infinitude of the divine perfections, that the voice of revelation confirms, that universal nature proclaims—so far, at least, as the finite is capable of witnessing to the Infinite. God is intelligible then, in His attributes as in Himself. Here rest contented; but beware of scrutiny! Be satisfied that by the aid of reason you may apprehend Him; but strive not to comprehend, or again comes the struggle, and the blinding with excess of light.

Or, ask questions, if you will, that you may hear in answer the mere stammerings and lispings of science, embarrassed by the inscrutable grandeur of its Object. Learn how that He endures without time; that He is immense without magnitude; intelligent without consciousness; Infinite, yet Personal; Manifold and yet One; Necessary and yet Free; simple but omnipresent; He is wholly in the whole, and yet wholly in each part of the universe; always equally present to times past, present, or future; ever ancient, ever young; unchangeable, yet all-changing; ever working, always at rest; He is jealous without anxiety; repents without grief; is calm in His indignation; He changes His work, His purpose unchanged; He seeks yet possesses all things; He requires the love of creatures, and yet is always sufficient for Himself, and ever sovereignly happy in His own self-blessedness.

Thus the very statements which reason compels us to make about the Almighty seem to be contradictory of one another. The contradiction arises from our imagination, which still colours with an earthly element our very loftiest conceptions. Reason rebukes, corrects, protests against the contradictoriness of imagination; it strives to reconcile, at least to postpone difficulties, which only recur again to hamper it afresh. At length it yields; the mind is wearied and oppressed; "Thy knowledge is become wonderful to me; it is high, and I cannot reach it." We gladly turn from the giddy thought of God to the works of His hands; He will be revealed in His works.

And here, again, on the surface is light and knowledge, in the depths wonder and amazement. "The heavens," indeed, "show forth the glory of God, and the firmament declareth the work of His hands."[1] "The firmament on high is His beauty, the beauty of heaven with its glorious show."[2] "Look upon the rainbow, and bless Him that made it; it is very beautiful in its brightness."[3] "O how desirable are all His works; and what we know is but a spark!"[4] From the cedar of Libanus to the hyssop that grows upon the wall—from the huge machinery of the heavens to the leaf of a tree, or smallest shell, or minutest insect—each great or small created thing is in itself a miracle of design. "Wonderful are Thy works," exclaims the Psalmist, "and that my soul knoweth right well!"[5] Wonderful, indeed; but so far at least intelligible that, whether the work be great or small, He works by rule and method; He contrives certain means to work out a certain preconceived design; and man himself, who is also, in

---

[1] Ps. xviii. 1. [2] Ecclus. xliii. 1. [3] Ibid. ver. 12.
[4] Ibid. xlii. 23. [5] Ps. cxxxviii. 14.

His Maker's image, an intelligent agent, enters into the plan and purpose of the Creator, detects the design, and judges the result. In so doing he is only acting the part of a rational being, measuring by intelligence the workmanship of infinite intelligence. And thus, of every work of God, he asks (it is only natural), Wherefore? to what wise and good end? with what useful and beneficial result? And then—for His ways are not as our ways, nor His thoughts as our thoughts—comes the conflict, the remonstrance and the disputation with God.

But what is this! you object, are, not all the works of God good and perfect in their kind; and all His ways are they not righteous and just? Doubtless, in themselves, and in His sight, they are so; but shall man justify, to his shallow understanding, all the works and ways of God? Look up to the heavens above, and upon the earth below, and into the waters underneath, and say what you behold. Above are vast globes, revolving according to fixed laws in the empty wildernesses of space; to what end they exist, whether or not inhabited, and, if so, by what kind of creatures, with what relations to other worlds, and to their Creator—these are matters of pure conjecture. Here the reason is only embarrassed; but when from these we turn to the works of the Almighty in our own world, wonder is changed into amazement. For only consider the waste of life (as it appears to us), the abortive productions, the abnormal growths, the unsightly forms, the seemingly aimless natures which abound by land and sea; and add to these the wild, curious, startling modes of animal or vegetable life with which science or travel has familiarised us—what shall we say? Oh, how different shows the God of nature from the God of reason, or the God of revelation, or the God that speaks in conscience! Certainly the spectacle of brute nature, in the lions and pards of the wilderness, or the monsters of the great deep, seems, at first sight, to find no place in the mind of the religious thinker. And yet these monsters divide the world with man; and the crust of the earth is the sepulchre of others more strange even than these, more hideous, more appalling. Sometimes it would almost seem that the God of nature had abandoned His work to the mere blind, fortuitous working of the living forces, or that another had usurped His place, so wild, so strange, so grotesque and extravagant even, appear to us a large portion of His inventions! And then they suffer; not merely the savage kinds, which are designed, in their very structure, to rend and devour one another, but gentle, affectionate creatures that draw near to man, and render him a willing service for use, or companionship, or sportive idleness. A man will almost weep over a tortured brute; and the God of nature, is He not concerned that they suffer?

Nor ought such reflections as these to disturb a simple, faithful mind which is habituated to the thought of God, even though they should present unanswerable difficulties. For the very statement that God is incomprehensible in His works, what does it mean, but that questions may be started concerning them, which, in our ignorance, we cannot answer? Hence, when it was permitted to holy Job to enter into judgment with his Maker, the Angel of the Lord did not answer his objections (else Job had missed his lesson), but questioned in turn, and shamed him in his ignorance. And, in like manner, the difficulties suggested in the contemplation of the natural world require, not so much an answer (though our feebleness may essay some sort of answer) as an *account*. And our ignorance is the account; our ignorance, and that which springs of ignorance, as the prejudice, the mental narrowness, the false colour with which the mind oftentimes invests an object, and the like.

Thus: if God seem sometimes strange in His works, yet it may well be that it is only the narrowness of our own minds that makes Him strange. We forget that He is infinite; we have been used to consider Him only in one light or aspect, until the mind has, unconsciously, taken a warp; when suddenly He reveals Himself in another and very different aspect, and we are unprepared for it, it takes us by surprise; when, deep as He is high, He stoops to revel, to *disport* in His work (if I may use a bold word, but one which has the warrant of Scripture[1]), out of the very freedom and happiness of His nature, and the boundless wealth and variety of the resources of His inventiveness; and so, to our narrowness, His

---

[1] Prov. viii. 30, 31.

very condescension, even like His awful Majesty, becomes a stumbling-block.

And it is a symptom, surely, of the same mental narrowness, if some brute creature, good in its kind, and the work of His hands, be hideous in our eyes, merely because it is curious, or an object of terror, because we do not understand it. No wonder the works of nature seem strange to us, if we regard them with the eyes of children. Or, if we are shocked because animals exhibit emotions and actions which in ourselves would be sinful, yet it is but an idle fancy which would ascribe to them either vice or virtue, since they have not a moral nature. Or again, if we marvel that they suffer, yet the marvel is born of ignorance. Unless the brute be quickened by some lower kind of soul (so to term it), it cannot suffer, and we might as well be concerned for an automaton; but if it have such soul for its animating principle, yet no man knows what it is, or whence, or what its possible future destiny, that it should suffer. The sufferings of our fellow-men may be advantageous to themselves, since it is written: "Blessed be they that mourn;" but He who considers the sparrow's fall, and who had compassion on the "many beasts"[1] of the doomed Nineveh, has He not likewise a beatitude of mourning for the brute, though we be ignorant of the nature and manner of it?

And to our ignorance also must be ascribed that which appears as wasteful or aimless in nature. As

---
[1] Jon. iv. 11.

if, forsooth, God were a son of man who needed thrift and husbandry! What if He scatter a thousand seeds that one may germinate; what if between world and world expand interspaces immeasurable of idle wilderness; what if a thousand planets lie waste and empty, for one that is furnished and peopled; what if He have sown the vault of heaven with stars, as the earth with flowers, for no other end than His glory and their own loveliness? He may well afford to be prodigal whose resources are infinite! Or, as if we had angels' eyes to scan His far-reaching purpose—was the primeval forest once to no purpose, though it bloomed and wasted ten thousand years in seeming idle luxuriance, which now, charred beneath our feet, is a storehouse of light and heat for thousands of ages and millions of populations? And so if, like holy Job, we dare to enter into judgment with our Maker, we are speedily put to shame in our ignorance, and must confess with him: "Therefore I have spoken unadvisedly, and on matters above measure exceeding my knowledge."[1]

. . . "One thing I have spoken which I wish I had not said, and another to which I will add no more."[2]

But imperfection and disorder in the natural world, or that which, to our ignorance, appears as imperfection and disorder, why have I so much as named such a thing before a spectacle quite as strange, but unspeakably more awful—the spectacle of misery and degradation, sin and passion, anguish and death in man, God's image? Yes, my brethren, the existence

[1] Job xlii. 3. [2] Ibid. xxxix. 35.

of evil; here at last is the great mystery which, sooner or later, forces itself upon the attention, but not perhaps, until, as in the case of Job, it has been driven home to us by actual suffering in our own person. Here is the great struggle with God in which, willingly or unwillingly, we must be vanquished. But why? What is the meaning of suffering, and wherefore death? Sin, it is answered, sin is the cause of suffering and death; they are at once its consequence and its punishment. But how should the All-wise, and All-good, Who created all things in order and harmony—how should He suffer the serpent's slimy trail to corrode and defile His work, making beauty hideous, and setting a cloud between the Face of God and the children of men? Thus the original difficulty recurs. The scheme of God's providence allowed and gave a place to evil, and evil exists. Enough: we must not dispute, for we cannot alter it; to submit is all that is left for us.

My brethren, have patience with me yet awhile; bear to contemplate this subject. Do not turn aside, but consider it—you *must* consider it. Within, without, and around is the daily strife with evil. You cannot escape anyhow; nor is there need; I would reconcile you to it. The thought of God, as revealed in the reason, terrifies, dazzles, and overwhelms the mind; the thought of God, as revealed in His works, amazes in its strangeness, or confounds us in our ignorance. We would fain rise up to know Him; but His Infinitude overpowers us. If, with the impetuosity of love, we remonstrate, we contend, His majesty disarms, His glory strikes us to the earth. It would seem that between the Infinite and the finite the gulf must ever remain impassable. Now see how He Himself has, as it were, spanned and bridged over the abyss; and whereas the creature cannot rise to the Creator, the Creator Himself has, in loving pity, stooped down to the creature, and raised him up to Himself. Since we cannot rightly know the Almighty by reason, or in His works, behold He has sent His well-beloved and only-begotten Son into the world, born of a woman. He shall declare Him: He shall teach us what God is.

Lo! then, He comes; but oh, still and ever incomprehensible, on earth as in heaven, what do we behold? Who is this that, in the dark and lonely night, white and trembling, the damps of death on His brow, His eyes dimmed with tears, His Face worn and haggard, with uplifted hands, pleads in prayer with the Father, yet bows unto His will, and the chalice that may not pass—the scourge, the thorny crown, the spear, the death-throes, and the consummation. It is the Son of God, who contends in the name of all, and for us all, that in weakness He may prevail, and through His death we may be redeemed to everlasting life. Here is still mystery if you will; but it is a mystery which, while it awes the mind, melts the heart; and it is a mystery which reconciles us to all other mysteries. What matter though darkness surrounds the throne of God, where He dwelleth in His high and holy place, since He has shown Himself in the sweet, gracious image of His only-begotten Son? What matter though ignorance often clouds our mind to detect His plan in creation, since He has revealed to us the heavenly scheme of His loving mercies towards ourselves in the redemption of Jesus Christ? What matter though suffering and labour and trial be our portion now, and death in prospect, if all the sufferings of this life "are not worthy to be compared with the glory to come, that shall be revealed in us;"[1] if He have robbed the grave of victory, and plucked the sting from death? Or, He who Himself drained all the cup of human anguish, and freely tasted every bitterness of death, think you He had not abolished pain and death, were such abolition an unmingled good; and were it not the very excellent cunning of the heart's mould that our keenest delights and dearest joy and solace are born of pain and tears, which makes it sweeter often to suffer and die with Him than to be "full and reign" with the children of this world? Nay, look on those, mouthed wounds, those weeping stripes, that unsufferable torment of the Cross, and say, if He who endured such pains to save sinners from hell, had not abolished the great pit itself, were not hell for sinners in the very nature of things; and could He have abolished it without denying Himself, and those dear perfections that make Him God.

In short, which of the works and ways of God does most offend our weakness, or offends at all, before

---

[1] Rom. viii. 18.

the heart-piercing thought of the crucified Saviour? Who that will contend with Him on this ground, can "answer Him one for a thousand?"[1] We cannot complain that He is too high for us, when He has stooped so low to win our hearts; or that He is a stranger in His everlasting attributes, since He is equally strange, but oh, how desirable, in those wounds that love has dealt upon Him; or that He has taken up evil into His scheme, since evil has proved to us the most unspeakable good. It has taught us to know and love Him, as otherwise, surely, we never could have known or loved Him: it has revealed to us, as if, the very heart of God. "Oh, truly necessary Adam's sin! Oh happy fault, that deserved to have such and so great a Redeemer!"[2] And now I see that the Cross, in some manner, explains the scheme of nature, suggesting, as it does, that not in each several part, but in the whole plan, consists the admirable order and beauty of creation; in which even that which is called evil, being duly ordained, and fittingly disposed, does more eminently commend the good.[3] But then, who shall explain the Cross?

Jesus, Lord, I cannot fathom Thee! This is the very motive of my adoration, the great argument and sweetest provocative of love, that the narrow

---

[1] Job ix. 3.
[2] From the "Exultet," read in the service of Holy Saturday.
[3] "Ex omnibus consistit universitatis admirabilis pulchritudo; in quâ etiam illud quod malum dicitur, benè ordinatum, et suo loco positum eminentiùs commendat bona."—S. Augustinus, *Enchiridion*, cap.

vessel of Thy creature's mind is no fitting measure, indeed, for Thee; that intellect cannot conceive, nor fancy dream, nor eloquence utter "what is the breadth and length and height and depth" of the greatness that Thou art, and of Thy charity "which surpasseth all knowledge."[1] None the less, like Thy shepherd servant, will I strive with Thee, till the day break and the shadows flee; nor will I let Thee go until Thou bless me; but I do not ask Thy Name, for I know that it is LOVE.

[1] Ephes. iii. 18, 19.

IV.

THE FALL OF PETER.

"Wherefore he that thinketh himself to stand, let him take heed lest he fall."—1 COR. x. 12.

IT was not appointed in the redemption wrought for us by our Saviour, Jesus Christ, that it should remove that weakness of nature which inclines us to sin, any more than that it should remove sickness or death, or other effects of the fall of Adam. We might ask, Why did not the death of Christ destroy in us the concupiscence of sin, as well as sin itself? or, for that matter, Why did it not destroy death? But if it be right to ask such questions, yet, at any rate, it ought to be a sufficient answer to them that this was not the will of God. He ordained otherwise, and, we may be sure, wisely so ordained. However, Holy Scripture gives us the reason why it was so ordained, viz., that the power of God might be perfected in our infirmity. Since this is the rule, as St. Paul concludes, the weaker we are the stronger we are. "When I am weak then am I strong," since the weaker in self the stronger in God.

Let us not then repine, brethren, because the gift of God to us is not other than it is. It might be higher without being better for ourselves. Lucifer fell with more than an angel's gifts and beauty, finding in his very gifts and beauty the occasion of his fall. Our first parents fell because, created in a nature only a little less than that of angels, they aspired to be like gods, knowing good and evil. Our weak nature, it is true, inclines us forcibly to evil; yet, when we fall, it is not so much because nature is weak, as because we trust in it, weak as it is, instead of relying on the strength of God. Such was the case, for instance, in the Fall of Peter, which is recorded in the Gospel for our instruction.

For Peter fell, and sad indeed was his fall; yet he fell not *away*, but to rise again secure, having learnt the lesson of his fall. He fell, not so much through malice (though some malice must be in every fall), as through weakness. But again he did not fall, merely because he was weak, but because he was unaware of his weakness. And lastly, God permitted this great fall in order to teach both him and ourselves the caution of the text, "Let him that thinketh himself to stand take heed lest he fall."

I am sure that if we were reading the gospel for the first time, we should be startled by the Fall of Peter. His is not by any means the sort of character we should expect to give way. His figure stands out the boldest in relief amongst the Twelve, because the features are so strongly marked that they take the light better. Surely we have a better knowledge of him than of the others. We may picture to ourselves St. John, for instance; but we know the very heart of Peter. While the others only think, he speaks; while they only speak, he acts. He is formed by nature to be the leader, and the others take their cue and tone from him. For instance, they always let him be their spokesman.

Other disciples, as Andrew, Philip, and Nathaniel, had from the first avowed their belief that Jesus was the Son of God; but when He required a confession of their faith, they were content to let Simon be their mouth-piece: "Thou art Christ, the Son of the living God."[1] And again when many disciples were staggered at the announcement of the Holy Eucharist, it was Simon Peter who made for the Twelve the exhaustive act of faith: "Lord, to whom shall we go? Thou hast the words of Eternal Life, and we have believed and have known that Thou art the Christ, the Son of God."[2] Faith, the insight into things spiritual, this was his especial gift from the Father of Lights. A strong will, undaunted courage, and an ardent, loyal disposition — these were his gifts by nature; but to be leader in a spiritual kingdom required a spiritual gift, without which all natural endowments would be useless; and this was the gift of faith: "Blessed art thou, Simon Bar-jona, because Flesh and Blood hath not

[1] Matt. xvi. 16.   [2] John vi. 69, 70.

revealed it to thee, but My Father Who is in heaven."[1] The first time that our Lord looked on Simon, that Eye that reads the hearts of men discerned the gift in him. He chose him for it, and signified to him the new name he was henceforth to go by. "And Jesus, looking upon him, said, 'Thou art Simon, the son of Jona: thou shalt be called Cephas, which is interpreted Peter."[2] The Rock, that was to be his name, as the strong foundation of Christ's kingdom upon earth, unshaken by every storm of earth or hell: "Thou art Peter, and upon this Rock I will build My Church, and the gates of hell shall not prevail against it."[3] But with his prerogatives I am not concerned here, or save only to show from what a height he fell.

Even if our Blessed Saviour had not marked the *faith* of Peter for special commendation, we could see for ourselves that his was no mere homage of the lips; he realised what he said. His words on the miraculous draught of fishes, "Depart from me, O Lord, for I am a sinful man," are the words of one who felt in his inmost heart, that he had to do with his Lord and his Judge. His faith is still conspicuous, even when infirmity mixes with the motive that exercises it; as when he asked leave to walk and meet Christ on the waters, or when he objected, "Lord, be it far from Thee," *i.e.*, to suffer and die; and when he protested, "Thou shalt never wash my feet," or "Though I should die together with Thee, I will not deny Thee." His words betray a defect,

---

[1] Matt. xvi. 17. [2] John i. 42. [3] Matt. xvi. 18.

it is true; but if he sometimes forgot "what spirit he was of," yet so did James and John, and the other disciples. If he understood not, yet which of them, at first, did understand the mystery of the Cross? If he was over-bold in his protest that he would rather die than deny his Master, yet the others said the same thing: "And in like manner also said they all."[1] They were noble words, had he only made them good. Is it that the smallest fault shows gross in him that he is singled out for rebuke where others are passed over? No, but Jesus had read from the first the heart of Peter, and He answered not so much his words, as his thoughts. Alas, our very virtues may betray us, unless they be guarded by a habitual self-distrust; and our weakness often lies in the very region of our greatest strength! How significant it is that Jesus suffered Peter to sink a moment as he walked upon the waves! He had learnt what he could do in God; but he had yet to learn how weak he was in himself. But our Lord rebuked him, you will say, for his "littleness of faith." Yes; for faith itself is imperfect, if, to the higher knowledge of God which it brings, be not added a deeper sense of our own insufficiency.

It is commonly said that no man becomes wicked on a sudden. True, if it means that no man becomes *depraved* on a sudden. But surely a man may fall on a sudden,—if for a single moment he loses hold of the hand of God. We shall have learnt nothing from the Fall of Peter if we have not learnt this;

[1] Mark xiv. 31.

it is the very lesson. The seeds of corruption are in the worthiest of us. They were in Peter from the beginning; and at each manifestation of them came the sad, unheeded rebuke of his Divine Master. But now, when the time of his great trial was at hand, the warning voice is loud, marked and unmistakable.

The disciples were seated at table at the Last Supper, and there had been some strife amongst them as to precedency, in which it would seem that Peter had taken a part. Jesus rebuked them for it, and then, turning to Peter, He said: "Simon, Simon, behold Satan hath desired to have you that he may sift you like wheat; but I have prayed for thee that thy faith fail not; and thou, being once converted, confirm thy brethren." "Lord," he answers shortly, but earnestly, "I am ready to go with Thee both into prison and to death."[1] And then, when Jesus forewarns them that "All you shall be scandalised in Me this night," "Peter, answering, said to Him: 'Although *all* shall be scandalised in Thee, *I* will never be scandalised.'"[2] Ah, here is the damning proof of Peter's presumption, his egotistical laudation of his own, and implied disparagement of others' constancy. If he sometimes spoke when he had better have held his peace; if his attitude was demonstrative; if he made himself too forward; if he protested louder than the others; yet, remember that he loved his Lord exceedingly, and out of the abundance of the heart the mouth speaketh; and his whole char-

[1] Luke xxii. 31-33. [2] Matt. xxvi. 31, 33.

acter was ardent and impulsive. But then, what word is this? "All the rest may be scandalised in Thee: possible; but I—I—impossible!" for that is the spirit of it. It is the climax: "And Jesus saith to him: 'Amen, I say unto thee, to-day, even this night, before the cock crow twice, thou shalt deny Me thrice.' But he," the text continues, "spoke the more vehemently: 'Although I should die together with Thee, I will not deny Thee."[1]

Had Peter pondered the words which our Blessed Saviour had just now spoken to him he had hardly slept that night. But, spite of remonstrance and warnings, his mind is at rest. Ah, how often is danger lurking close in our hour of fancied security! And so it is with Peter, who, together with James and John, is sleeping in the Garden, while their Lord is on his bitter watch. Twice He rouses them, "Simon, sleepest thou? Couldst thou not watch one hour? Watch ye and pray, lest ye enter into temptation."[2] The night is advanced, and their eyes are heavy; but oh, it is no time to sleep for them, and least of all for Peter. He would not hear; he would not be warned; at least let him pray. Satan wakes while Peter sleeps; and the hour of trial and darkness is at hand. In vain! The warning is unheeded, like the rest. So He comes at length the third time, and in very bitterness of heart bids them "Sleep ye now, and take your rest. It is enough. The hour is come, and the Son of Man shall be betrayed into the hands of sinners."[3]

[1] Mark xiv. 30, 31. [2] Ibid. vers. 37, 38. [3] Ibid. ver. 41.

There is a stir, a tramp of footsteps in the Garden, a hushed murmur of voices, and the gleam of lanthorns through the trees. It is Judas Iscariot, and his coming would seem peaceful; but there is a wild boding in his eye, as he salutes the Master; and the men with him are armed with clubs and staves. His salute was a signal, and, shortly, rough hands are laid on the Lamb of God. Peter is now roused in earnest. There is a scuffle, and a voice cries, "Lord, shall we strike with the sword?"[1] But it is not the voice of Peter, for he has struck already, without leave-asking; when the Lord interposes, bids him sheathe his weapon, with a word heals the wounded man; and then with a calm remonstrance on the violence of their manner, He commits Himself at once into the rude keeping of the band, who bind and lead Him on to the house of Caiphas.

The disciples, in fear for themselves, now made off; but not so Peter. He was no coward, and he was armed; and besides, had he not said: "I am ready to go with Thee into prison and to death." He followed then, but with a slack pace; he "followed," we read, "afar off!"[2] Is this Peter? When from his boat he should see Jesus standing on the shore, he would cast himself into the sea and swim ashore, out of his impatience to greet Him. He ran with John to the Sepulchre, on the tidings of the Resurrection, though John outran him. Why is he so tardy now, when, if ever, his place should be at his Master's side? His slack pace is the sign of a slack, irresolute

[1] Luke xxii. 49. [2] Matt. xxvi. 58.

mind. He would have fought to the death; but the voluntary surrender of Jesus, that it is which has unnerved and unsettled him. His pace is slack, for he has begun to walk in a path which is new and dark to him—the way of the Cross. His pace is slack, for he is thinking, and on what is to be the end? "And Peter followed afar off, even to the house of the High Priest . . . that he might see the end." His pace is slack, for there is *One* at his side who is breathing a word into his ear, to which if once he hearkened, he would never follow more, however slackly, in the footsteps of Jesus Christ. He never listened to it for a single moment; we have his Master's word for that: "Satan hath desired to have you, that he might sift you like wheat; but I have prayed for thee that thy faith fail not." So he follows on however slackly to the house of Caiphas.

The trial had already begun, while Peter was kept waiting in an outer court, until the word of a disciple who was known to the High Priest gained him admittance into the palace. Once entered, Peter seeks a place where he can learn what is said and done, without thrusting himself into notice; for he has not come to bear a part, but "to see the end." The spring air is chilly; and in the midst of the lower court, or hall adjoining the trial-chamber, there is a pan of coals, with a mixed group of servants and officials circled round it. These Peter joins; for he is cold, and he will hear what is doing, or has been done.

They are discussing the cause in which he is so narrowly concerned. These underlings reflect the tone of their betters, and it is unfavourable to Jesus. Peter is now in the presence of an enemy far more subtle and dangerous than the armed gang who had assailed his Master. These he would have dealt with after their kind; but here is quite another kind of foe, against which another sort of courage is required —the public opinion of the capital! He hears their talk: he listens eagerly. Ah, the bravest spirit, the surest judgment, the safest innocence can hardly hear unmoved the adverse voice of opinion! It has made the boldest tongue to falter, and innocence itself to blush like guilt. And then so little self-reliant are we by nature, that our most cherished convictions seem to waver, when unsupported by the sweet approbation of others. The disciples had fled: Jesus stands before the Tribunal, self-surrendered, silent, like a criminal! The world has already anticipated judgment, and has passed its verdict against Him; and Peter stands alone. Downcast he was before; but now depression has given way to a new sensation, which makes his ears burn and tingle while he listens: he is *ashamed!* The World is the last of the three enemies of our salvation that we care to arm ourselves against; and Peter had not armed *himself* against it; he had plunged into the very danger.

"Thou also wast with Jesus of Nazareth," said a voice at his side. It was the maid who had let him in who made the charge. What was it to her, who he was, or where, or with whom he had been? How sudden temptation is, sometimes, but then it is often our own fault that it is sudden. Peter might have expected this: could he think to pass unnoticed amongst the crowd, and unchallenged, he who had borne so prominent a part as a disciple? And then his is not the face I think, which, once seen, a man easily forgets. "I neither know nor understand what thou sayest," he mutters, with strange, altered voice. "And he went forth before the court."[1]

As he drew thus nearer to Jesus and the trial, did he hear the cock crow? *Once!* and before the idle tongue of a gossiping maid! But he will not escape; for presently other eyes and tongues are busied about him, and a man this time accosts him, repeating the charge, that "Thou also art one of them." "O man, I am not;"[2] and "he denied with an oath,"[3] for it vexes him to the soul to have to repeat the shameful lie. *Again!*—He would, and *we* would, fain stop at the first sin; but then there is, mostly, just the same reason for the second, or third sin as for the first.

A short breathing time, about an hour's space,[4] is granted, during which Peter is let alone, to look, if, for very shame he dares look, on the mock trial of the Son of God; or worse, to look into his own soul and see the fearful change that is there! Then Satan is at work with him again. And there came other of the bystanders charging him, amongst the rest a kinsman of Malchus, whose ear he had cut off, who asks, "Did I not see thee with Him in the Garden?" Then began Peter "to curse and to swear that he

[1] Mark xiv. 67, 68. [2] Luke xxii. 58.
[3] Matt. xxvi. 72. [4] Luke xxii. 59.

knew not the Man."[1] Hark the cock-crow, clear and shrill, piercing his soul like the voice of the accusing Angel! *Thrice!*—" And the Lord turning looked on Peter." [2]

He looked not on him in wrath. Oh no, Peter could have better borne the flash of indignation than the sad, loving, reproachful gaze that met his own! Peter had disowned Jesus, but Jesus had not disowned Peter. Then the divine glance lighted up every corner of his soul like the lightning flash. While he saw Jesus, Jesus showed him himself; and he is changed in a moment. Oh, sweet, bitter, piercing remorse of grace! He is ready to swoon between love and grief. The solemn spectacle swims around his eyes. He pushes aside the crowd, who wonder what ails the man. They are nothing to him now. He must get him without—into the night. He must be alone, quite alone. He has a word to say in God's own ear, if only he can say it, out of the swoln heart-grief that struggles in his throat. Pardon, sweet Jesus!—There, in the palace garden, amidst the dews of the morning twilight, bowed to the earth, shaken with convulsive sobs, knocking his breast, wringing his hands, groaning in the agony of his soul, lies the Rock, the Head, the Mouth-piece, the President of the Apostolic College!

Peter is fallen! Tremble, proud brother, who, wrapped in the haughtiness of an ungodly self-respect, in the absence of temptation, would laugh to scorn the bare suggestion that such as you could

[1] John xviii. 26; Matt. xxvi. 74.   [2] Luke xxii. 61.

ever be capable of meanness or disgrace! Tremble, ungentle sister, severe in virtue, to bruise the broken reed and quench the smoking flax! Let all be warned by the great example.

And now, brethren, mark the sequel of this sad but instructive history. The sacred drama hastens on to its accomplishment; but without Peter. Not when Jesus was tried before Pilate, not when He was flouted with purple rag and thorny crown and cane sceptre; not in the weary ascent of Calvary, did eye of friend or foe mark out Simon Peter's hard-lined face amongst the throng. Was this kind, was this worthy? More worthy, think you, to strike, even yet, a clumsy unavailing blow with the sword? Or, since that was forbidden, rush boldly into the throng, and cry, unsaying his base denial: Hold, hold off your hands, men; ye know not what ye do. It is the Son of God whom ye would crucify: I say it—I, Simon who denied Him. But I was weak, I was mad: I am ready to die with Him! That were indeed a brave part; but, remember that in the way of bravery Peter had well nigh met his ruin. Sad indeed, not to stand at the foot of the Cross, together with Mary and Magdalen and Salome, and his fellow-apostle St. John; but had Peter stood there, he had not learnt his lesson nor taught it us, that in spiritual matters cowardice is often the highest bravery.

And now that Peter has learnt to distrust himself, Jesus will trust Peter,—to feed both lambs and sheep, to govern the whole Church of God, according to the sacred charge which He gave him after He was risen from the dead. And if while He entrusted him, He gently, at the same time, reminded him of his sin, it was only that thereby it might be manifest to all how genuine and thorough was the change which Grace had wrought in his heart: "Simon, son of John, lovest thou Me more than these?" "Yea, Lord," he answers, "Thou knowest that I love Thee."—But *more than these?* for that was the question. No, no, he will not say that *now;* he knows to his cost that that way lies ruin and disgrace. Then the question is repeated, but without the comparative "more than these," a second, and a third time. Ah, what is the meaning? "And Peter was grieved because He said to him the third time, 'Lovest thou Me.' And he said to Him, 'Lord, Thou knowest all things; Thou knowest that I love Thee.'"[1] When the meaning broke upon him, his eyes would overflow afresh, but they were sweet tears. Thrice an act of love for thrice denied! Oh, it was his love that saved him.

Let us, brethren, learn from his example, that he who truly loves his Lord will never be suffered to go far astray; but oh, let us also learn that love is better shown by deeds than by words, however sincerely spoken they may seem to be, and that even love itself is unsafe, unless it be guarded by an abiding self-distrust. Let us watch and pray, that we enter not into temptation, and ever shun the path of danger, especially where our ruling passion is concerned. Let us always, if indeed we know our own weakness, compassionate our neighbour's lapses, "considering

[1] John xxi. 15, 16, 17.

ourselves, lest we also be tempted."[1] Let us beware how we think ourselves to stand, for temptation will come, and Pride ever goes before a fall! But if, weak and fickle as we are, we should in any rash moment vainly trust ourselves, do not Thou trust us, but, Lord, save us ere we perish! Hold us up by Thy hand of grace, lest we be merged in the gulf of sin and passion. And though we should have forgotten Thee, alas! do not Thou, sweet Jesus, forget us, but turn and look on us, as on Peter, and we shall turn and look on Thee. Show us only the light of Thy Countenance to our salvation, and we shall not care to look on vanity to our everlasting undoing.

[1] Gal. vi. 1.

V.

THE FACE OF GOD.

"Turn not away Thy Face from me, lest I be like unto them that go down into the pit."—Ps. cxlii. 7.

WE read much in Holy Scripture to the effect that man cannot, in this life, see God: "Thou canst not see My Face," He said to Moses, "for man shall not see Me and live."[1] And yet there is a sense in which the just are said to see God in this life, and to behold the Light of His Countenance. Indeed, in the very chapter in which God declares to Moses that he cannot see His Face, we read these words, "My Face shall go before thee, and I will give thee rest."[2] And again, the Psalmist says, "The Light of Thy Countenance, O Lord, is signed upon us: Thou hast given gladness in my heart."[3] ... "Thou hast made known to me the ways of life; Thou shalt fill me with joy with Thy Countenance."[4] ... "Thou hast set our iniquities

---

[1] Exod. xxxiii. 20.   [2] Ibid. ver. 14.
[3] Ps. iv. 7.   [4] Ibid. xvi. 11.

before Thine eyes; our life in the Light of Thy Countenance."[1] . . . "Make Thy Face to shine upon Thy servant: save me in Thy mercy."[2] . . . "Neither did their own arm save them, but Thy Right Hand, and Thine Arm, and the Light of Thy Countenance."[3] And, in the words of the Text, "Turn not away Thy Face from me, lest I be like unto them that go down into the pit."

Passages of this kind, perhaps you will tell me, brethren, are figurative, and so indeed they are: it is a method used by the Holy Spirit, in Scripture, to instruct by figures; and so it were folly to pass over what is here said about the Face of God and the Light of His Countenance, without asking ourselves what is meant by the figure—what it is a figure of? And in answering this question, I hope to find matter at once instructive and practical, and suitable for this present season of Lent.

It was given, at sundry times, to the ancient patriarchs and prophets, to see God under the guise and semblance of an angel speaking in the divine Person; but from the words used, it is clear that the passages just now quoted refer, not to such exceptional manifestations of the glory of God, but to some personal good and blessing of the spiritual life. Man may be said, again, to see God, as it were, by the light of nature, even: but the manner of this vision is dark, and its object could scarcely be called the Face of God; unless indeed to the light of nature be added the Light of Grace.

[1] Ps. lxxxix. 8.   [2] Ibid. xxx. 17.   [3] Ibid. xliii. 4.

Neither could this kind of knowledge be said to fill us with joy, to gladden our hearts, and give us rest and peace.

For you know, brethren—such amongst you as are familiar with them—how cold and comfortless are the school-proofs for the existence of God. Not that I mean to disparage them, or in aught detract from their usefulness in their proper sphere; much less, after the fashion of the day, and in accordance with a false philosophy, to deny their validity: God forbid! He has written upon the heavens above, and upon the earth beneath, and within our own souls, that which witnesses to Him, in order that no flesh which disowns Him may be held excused in His sight. But certainly, of all the ways in which man may be said to see God, in this life, that of seeing Him by the mere light of unaided intellect is the poorest and lowest. And hence it is that so little effect is produced by such controversialists as address themselves, not to the heart, but to the mere intellect of the unbeliever; and that intellect blinded, it may be, as we know it is capable of being blinded, as the result of a criminal life.

Since, then, the Face of God is not that of an angel bearing the name of God, nor the Mind and Power of God revealed in external nature, nor His witness written in the human intellect, in what sense can man be said, even while on earth, to see God, and be gladdened by the Light of His Countenance?

Brethren, you will have anticipated, indeed I have

already told you the answer: it is by the supernatural light of divine grace that the soul sees God. It is the Holy Spirit of God, Who indwells in our hearts by grace, that shows us the Face of God. This was the blessing with which the High Priest, in the Old Law, was instructed to bless the people of Israel, as though in it all other spiritual blessings were included: "The Lord bless thee, and keep thee: the Lord show His Face to thee, and have mercy on thee: the Lord turn His Countenance to thee, and give thee peace."[1] And yet this was, after all, only a pledge and anticipation, a prophecy of future good things in the Church which the Jewish system typified: it is to Christians that is given the fulness of the benediction. For God revealed His Face to the children of Israel in effect and operation only. It was the visitations of His Grace which were to them, as it were, the Face of God, and the Light of His Countenance; but to us is given the very indwelling in our souls of the Holy Spirit Himself, Who is the Source and Fountain of grace, as St. Paul witnesses: "He that raised up Jesus Christ from the dead shall quicken also your mortal bodies, because of His Spirit that dwelleth in you."[2] And again, he says that, "The Spirit Himself giveth testimony to our spirit, that we are the sons of God."[3]

Do not then misunderstand me, brethren. In this vision one does not frame before the imagination any sort of picture of what God is: impossible! The object of the vision is neither bodily shape, nor intel-

[1] Numb. vi. 24-26. [2] Rom. viii. 11. [3] Ibid. ver. 16.

lectual conception; it is *with the eyes of the heart*[1] (to use a Scripture phrase), and not with the mental eye, that the Face of God is seen. What is meant is this —that there is given to just men a sense of God's presence within their hearts, which is so plainly felt and discerned by them, that it is as if they saw Him. And what wonder, since God, as we have just now seen, does actually indwell in the hearts of the just through His Holy Spirit! Could He so indwell without giving them some quite unmistakable token of His presence? No, my brethren, I appeal to your own hearts; for they will bear witness to the truth of what I say. The just man has a real sense of God, as a reality, which grows with his spiritual growth. He is not merely, as the heathen may be, persuaded that there is a God; he does not merely believe, as the unjust may also believe, that there is a God: he *knows* it. It is hardly more plain to him that there is a sun in the sky, or that he has eyes and limbs, than that there is a God. And it is significant, from this point of view, that our Blessed Lord tells His disciples that "the world cannot receive" the "Spirit of Truth," because "it *seeth Him not*, nor knoweth Him;" while He adds, "but you shall know Him, because He shall abide with you, and shall be in you."[2]

But I do not mean to say that this spiritual sense of the presence of God, in which He shows His Face to just men, is given to all of them in equal keenness and intensity, or that the same person, how holy

[1] Eph. i. 18.   [2] John xiv. 17.

soever he may be, enjoys the gift at all times in equal keenness and intensity. Of course not: this would be to contradict all experience. When our spirit is ruffled or disturbed, when one is immersed in the bustle and turmoil of worldly affairs, or excited, or distracted, or amused—then, it is true, the Presence is unnoticed; and yet even so (it may be) we are aware that it is there; just as, while we are in company with an earthly friend, we may be, for some moments, so preoccupied and wrapt in our own thoughts, as not to notice his presence, and yet have, at the same time, a sort of under-consciousness that he is there all the while. And in the same way, when one is unwell, or in pain, or anguish of mind, or in spiritual desolation and dereliction, the soul feels, and perhaps complains to God, that His Face is clouded to her; yes, but He is there by the very token that His Face is clouded; it is because she *knows* that He is there that she complains that He clouds His Face.

At other seasons, as when our best mostly prevails over our worst self; or at God's own times, when He foresees that it will be profitable to us; oftentimes in the night, when the eyes of the body are darkened, the Face of God shines out clearly before the spiritual gaze; and as it is expressed in Holy Writ, the just "rejoice in their beds,"[1] and "the night is light as the day."[2] For they feel that God is there, and they could surely see Him, if His nature were of the quality of things that can be seen with the eyes of the body.

[1] Ps. cxlix. 5.   [2] Ps. cxxxviii. 12.

So that, supposing all the school-proofs of a divine Being were wanting, or that, as is sometimes pretended, they could all be argued as inconclusive, it is quite certain that a good and holy man would be little affected by the discovery. He to whom God is present in the heart wants not to have it proved to him that there is a God. And while God is thus a reality to the just, so is He to the perfect, the only reality worth living for. And while the wicked would be only too glad if they could persuade themselves that there was no God; while they are in some cases so foolish as to profess unbelief as to His existence—like the fool in Scripture who "hath said in his heart, 'There is no God;'"[1] it is certain, on the other hand, that to the just, or at any rate, to one who has lived habitually in the practice of a holy life, it would be simply a hell to entertain the very notion that there was no such being as God. To such a one everything that is less than God, has become in comparison vain and unreal; and without Him life itself would be intolerable.

But while the vision of God is thus the privilege of the just, our Blessed Saviour, in the gospel, declares it to be especially the blessing of the *clean* of *heart:* "Blessed are the clean of heart, for they shall see God." And though these words were spoken of the happy vision of God in Heaven, yet, since the just do see God in this life, in the sense explained, it is scarcely a mere adaptation of their meaning to apply them to the present subject. The beatitude is naturally

[1] Ps. xiii. 1.

double; the vision upon earth being, in its measure, a foretaste of the vision of Heaven; and it is the same blinding vice which chiefly disqualifies for the one and for the other.

And this being the case, to come to that practical application which the treatment of the subject has naturally led me into, what should I say to you, brethren, by way of warning against such a vice, should you be tempted, or which, God forbid, should you be unhappily entangled in it? Shall I remind you of the law whereby each sin is punished, chiefly, in that kind in which it had been offended; and that, consequently, even in this life, be sure your sin will find you out, and the abuse of the senses be followed by the punishment of the senses? Shall I tell how the sin goes to destroy all energy of character, blunts the edge of the intellect, ruins the finest faculties, deadens the affections, and degrades and brutalises the whole man? Shall I add that, besides the sin being its own punishment, God has added other punishments? Shall I speak of the special punishments whereby He has visited the offender in this life, and added the remembrance of the unquenchable fire which is reserved for it in the next? No, no: it is sufficient to have mentioned these considerations; but it is unnecessary to dwell upon them. The fear of God is only the beginning of wisdom. There are men in the world whom one may and must threaten with the divine vengeance; it is the only argument which would influence them. But these, surely, know not God as you have been taught to know Him.

More profitable for you, the words of my text: "Turn not away Thy Face from me, lest I be like unto them that go down into the pit." Compared with such a motive as this, what is pain or pleasure, health or sickness, intelligence or incapacity—all the goods or all the ills of life combined?

Oh, my brethren, may you never know (if indeed you have never known it) what kind of hell it is when God hides His Face, and the soul rejoices no more in the Light of His Countenance! I speak not of what is commonly called remorse. The loathing when the pleasure palls, the sickness of heart which follows on excess, the disquietude of mind, and anger with oneself; and, above all, the rule of God written in the reason, which condemns the crookedness of the sinner's ways; all this is remorse. The heathen whose soul has never known the indwelling of the Holy Spirit, and "the peace which passeth understanding," can feel the sentiment as keenly as the Christian, and as aptly describe it. It has been, in all ages, a commonplace topic of the poet and the moralist. But oh, it is something more than remorse which is at the bottom of that bitter heart-ache, and which prompts the inward, loud cry, as of him who had sold his birthright! What it is let the Psalmist tell, who knew well both what God is, and what it is to lose Him: "The enemy hath persecuted my soul," he says; "he hath brought down my life to the earth. He hath made me to dwell in darkness, as those who have been dead of old; and my spirit is in anguish within me, my heart within me is troubled. I remembered the days of old; I meditated on all Thy works, I meditated on the works of Thy Hands. I stretched forth my hands to Thee: my soul is as earth without water unto Thee. Hear me speedily, O Lord! my spirit hath fainted away. Turn not away Thy Face from me, lest I be like unto them that go down into the pit."

Yes, my brethren, in this world, as in the next, it is the hiding from us of God's Face, the Pain of Loss, as divines have termed it, which gives to sin its own peculiar sting. Mere pain one may learn to bear; but how will you endure to lose the Face of God? Absalom, unworthy as he was, could not bear to be banished from his father's face. He asked only to see him—and die if it must be—but to see him. "I beseech thee," he said to Joab, "that I may see the face of the king; and if he be mindful of mine iniquity, let him slay me."[1] But to lose the sight of God, to be a banished man from Him, what balm is there for a heart-wound like this? Will you strive to console yourself for your loss with the good things of this world? Then will you be disappointed. Without God, you will find you cannot even so much as enjoy the blessings of this world. For what is it that sheds a glory on the things of earth, but, in the language of holy Job, *the Lamp of God shining overhead?*"[2] And when, instead of the Lamp of God, there is darkness overhead, what is all the world but thorns and brambles, dust and ashes, vanity and vexation of spirit?

[1] 2 Kings xiv. 32. [2] Job xxix. 3.

Or, supposing that without God you could truly relish the joys of life, yet what a paltry satisfaction it would be after all! For what earthly good, what occupations, what pursuits or pleasures, what companionship of friends could ever stand you in His stead? Robbed of Him, with that bandage of sin over your eyes, with that heart-ache at the breast, what more would be wanting to complete your Hell, but eternal duration? Other torments it has, I do not forget them; but to be void of God were surely a hell in itself.

There are men in the world, I know, who cannot feel this; they would count the language which I hold to you as idle words; or, at any rate, they would consider it as exaggerated and unreal. They have not *lost* God, so of course they cannot feel the loss: they never knew Him; or, if once they knew Him, yet long practice in sin has not only blinded them, but reconciled them to their blindness. There will be a terrible opening of the eyes one day, for such as these. They do not see God indeed, for they do not see spiritual truths at all. Spiritual truths are spiritually discerned; and they have not the Spirit. "The sensual man," says the Apostle, "perceiveth not those things that are of the Spirit of God; for they are foolishness to him, and he cannot understand."[1]

Far otherwise with you, my brethren, who have known and tasted of the divine gift; in whose souls God indwells, through His Spirit,—your conscience

[1] 1 Cor. ii. 14.

bears witness to my words; you have clean hearts to see God. But you will only see Him clearly (this, I know) in proportion as you shall have kept your hearts unstained. Oh, if it be that you have ever sinned in that kind which chiefly darkens, pray for light! If it be that you see indeed, but only dimly; that you have not that keen sense of the reality of God and the unseen world, and of the evil of sin, which you ought to have; that the present world which passes seems, on the contrary, more real in your eyes than God and the world to come, pray for light! If it be that the consciousness of having trifled with your soul, and the shame consequent thereupon, have not indeed banished, but grieved the Holy Spirit of God, "whereby you are sealed unto the day of redemption,"[1]—not indeed darkened, but veiled the Face of God; in such sort that you see Him, as it were, through a cloud,—pray for light: "Enlighten," O Lord, "mine eyes that I may never sleep in death!"[2] And may the Father of Lights chase away the shadows of night, and dispel all the mists and vapours of sin and shame. May the Lord bless us and keep us, to-day and for evermore. May He show us His face, and have mercy on us. May He turn towards us the Light of His Countenance and give us peace—even the peace which passeth understanding! May He never cast us away from His Face, nor take His Holy Spirit from us! May this glorious reality of the Face of God grow daily before the eyes of our soul, and shine out in strength

---

[1] Eph. iv. 30. [2] Ps. xii. 3.

and gladness, until it be lost in the full vision and fruition of Him in Heaven: no longer an earnest, but satiety; no longer a figure, but the Substance; no longer with the eyes of the heart, but Face to face; when we shall know even as we are known, and, "in His Light, shall see light!"[1]

[1] Ps. xxxv. 10.

VI.

THE CALL OF PILATE.

"And Pilate seeing that he prevailed nothing, but that rather a tumult was made, taking water washed his hands before the people, saying, 'I am innocent of the blood of this just Man: look you to it.'"—MATT. xxvii. 24.

TO every one is given his Call of Grace from the Father of Lights, and on the answer to that call may depend his condition for everlasting. The manner and circumstances of the call differ with different persons. To some greater, to others less grace is given; but where much has been given, much also will be required. While some are called, in a manner, all their lives through, others are called chiefly once; and the grace thus offered, if rejected, may never be offered again. We may be required, in any hour, to take a decided step to the right hand or to the left; and our eternal happiness may depend on the decision.

This train of thought is suggested to me on reading the gospel account of Christ's trial before Pilate. For Pilate also had his hour of grace: the whole narrative shows how powerfully he was moved by it. He indeed was called, and on a sudden, to listen to the voice of God, which spoke in his conscience, as also to his outward senses, or else to be made partaker in a crime which, from the very nature of the case, is unparalleled in the annals of crime. And his conduct under the trial which I am now going to consider, is instructive, and may well serve as an example of warning to ourselves.

Pilate then, worldling and sceptic as he was, had never succeeded, like so many other men of his stamp, in stifling within his breast the voice of conscience. His conscience spoke to him very plainly, and he did not quite disregard its admonitions. On the contrary, this was the homage that he paid to virtue, to approve the right course; to wish, desire, and strive that justice should prevail; and then, though yielding at length under the pressure of temptation, yet to yield against his inclinations, and under protest. And this mode of conduct led him into a very curious but not uncommon self-deception. Because he hearkened to the voice of conscience, without however obeying its dictates; because every best and generous feeling of his nature was enlisted on the right side, he therefore deemed himself innocent. And though he himself gave the word which condemned the Holy One to the Cross, yet he washed his hands of His blood. In short, he *tampered* with his conscience. And in so saying, understand, brethren, distinctly what I mean. We are said to tamper with a thing when we use it in a manner in which it was never intended to be used. Now the voice of conscience, which is God's command in our breast, is not to be merely applauded, or shirked, or argued with, or paltered with, but to be obeyed.

But now let us turn to the sacred narrative, and see if it does not bear out this view of Pilate's conduct; and also that we may realise, in all its bearings, the solemn power of the call which he rejected. Let me first briefly preface the dread event :—

Jesus, having been condemned before the High Priest and the Sanhedrim, on the charge of blasphemy, in that He had "made Himself the Son of God," the Jews now led Him before the Roman Governor, Pontius Pilate, that He might be sentenced to death. But of the crime of blasphemy, though capital according to Jewish law, the Roman court would not take cognisance; so the charge preferred before Pilate was, not of blasphemy, but of treason and sedition: He perverted the nation (they said); He forbade to pay tribute; He made Himself King of the Jews. His authority thus invoked, the Governor enters the Judgment Hall, while the Jews await the verdict from without (for they would not enter the Hall, lest they might incur legal defilement, and so be unable to eat the Passover). He goes before the very Source and Fountain of grace; He goes to be confronted with One whose very Presence and aspect searched the hearts of men and brought sinners on their knees; He goes to judge his Judge.

Jesus therefore stands before Pilate. Holy pictures

have preserved to us the main outlines of the sacred Humanity of God the Son. Pilate would see in the supposed criminal the form, stately and gracious, of One in the bloom of Manhood, once fair and comely above the sons of men; but now His Countenance is "as it were hidden;" for the coming Cross has already overcast it with its rueful shadow. The gentle, patient eyes are dimmed with watching and tears; and the last night's superhuman agony and blood-sweat have left their ghastly traces on the haggard brow and sunken cheeks. And He bears upon Him the marks of the rough handling, the blows and the spittings which He had received in the Hall of Caiphas. He looks like one already sealed for the doom of death.

Pilate's first emotion was one of surprise. He had expected to see a common malefactor, but the very sight of Jesus gave the lie at once to the charges brought against Him. "Art *Thou* the King of the Jews?" he asks. "My Kingdom is not of this world," is the answer. "If My Kingdom were of this world, My servants would certainly strive that I should not be delivered to the Jews; but now My Kingdom is not from hence." "Art Thou a King, then?" asks Pilate again. He is evidently interested. Could he —could any man, think you, look unmoved on the Face of Jesus Christ, even in the hour of His humiliation? Had not the Call of Grace already begun to exercise him? "Art Thou a King, then?"—Yes, He was a King; for the phrase, "Thou sayest," was equivalent to plain Yes. "Thou sayest that I am a

THE CALL OF PILATE.

King: for this was I born, and for this came I into the world, that I should give testimony to the truth. Every one that is of the Truth heareth My Voice." "What is Truth?"[1] asks Pilate. And he turned away. Here was no malefactor, clearly, but a harmless dreamer, who thought to set up amongst men a Kingdom of Truth, forsooth, of which He Himself was to be the head, and all earnest truth-seekers His subjects. However this might be, on one thing his mind, he thought, was made up. He would be no tool of the Jews in this matter; he would be no party to the shedding of innocent blood. So he went out upon the balcony, and delivered his sentence to the expectant crowd—a simple verdict of acquittal: "I find no cause in Him."

It is easy to be honest in the absence of temptation; but sooner or later the temptation will come. Pilate might have expected that his verdict would be little welcome to the Jews; for "he knew that out of envy they had delivered Him up to him"— "Find no cause in Him!" Why, "He stirreth up the people, teaching throughout all Judea, beginning from Galilee to this place."[2] Jesus was a Galilean then! Gladly Pilate caught at this opportunity of shifting from himself a serious responsibility. There was no cause then to imbrue his hands in this innocent blood; no call to provoke the Jews, whom he had good reason to fear. The case belonged to Herod's jurisdiction, and to Herod should be referred.

[1] John xviii. 33, 36–38.   [2] Luke xxiii. 5.

So Jesus was sent before Herod, "who himself was at Jerusalem in those days." But Herod only treated the case as a jest; for a rival to the crown of Judea such as Jesus of Nazareth seemed to him beneath contempt: "Herod, with his army, set Him at nought, and mocked Him, putting on Him a white garment,"[1] and so sent Him back whence He had come; and the difficulty returns on Pilate's hands. Gladly also, oftentimes, would we ourselves shirk our responsibilities. But it may not be. No man can escape the probation whereby he is proved under the sun.

Pilate therefore comes out again before "the chief priests and the magistrates and the people." His words are grave, but there is weakness in his heart. He repeats his former verdict: "Behold, I have examined Him, and find no cause in this Man, in those things wherein you accuse Him. No, nor Herod neither; for I sent you to him, and behold, nothing worthy of death is done to Him."[2] That is the sentence; but he dares not act upon it at once, without fear or favour. He has an expedient by which, he thinks, he will at once both release Jesus and satisfy the Jews. "I find no cause in Him," he repeats, "but you have a custom that I release unto you one at the Pasch. Will you, therefore, that I release unto you the King of the Jews?" But the proposal is received with a shout of disfavour: "Not this man," they cry, "not this man, but Barabbas."[3] Then he remonstrates; that is, he argues with his tempters; and to argue with temptation is already

---

[1] Luke xxiii. 7, 11. [2] Ibid. ver. 13-15. [3] John xviii. 38-40.

half to yield : "Why, what evil hath this man done? I find no cause of death in Him. I will chastise Him therefore and let Him go."[1] What? chastise Him, when He had done no evil! Oh, Pilate has yielded too far already.

But just when the Tempter is busy with him, the Call of Grace comes again, and in power. For, even while he was now sitting in the judgment-seat, a message found him from his wife, saying: "Have thou nothing to do with that just man; for I have suffered many things this day in a dream because of Him."[2] A guilty conscience is startled at such a trifle as the fall of a leaf; but was this a trifle? Was it not rather a warning from Heaven, answering to the warning voice in his own breast? His next action shows how deeply he was moved: "Pilate, seeing that he prevailed nothing, but that rather a tumult was made, took water and washed his hands, saying: 'I am innocent of the blood of this just Man: look *you* to it.'" "His Blood be upon us and on our children!" they cry in awful, unwitting prophecy. And so Pilate delivered up the sacred Victim to that fearful scourging, which, according to the Roman custom, was the prelude to death by crucifixion.

But Pilate had really no intention of carrying out the sentence to the point of death. The scourging, he thought, was a concession with which the Jews ought to be satisfied; and it would be as he had said: "I will chastise Him and let Him go." The

---

[1] Luke xxiii. 22.   [2] Matt. xxvii. 18.

sinner always says to himself, "Thus far, but no farther: I will commit one sin, but not another. I will not stain my conscience with a blacker dye;" but ever, like the Jews, the rabid passions clamour for more. Oh, no doubt, Pilate's mind was made up, he would think, when he led Jesus back again, still quivering from the lash, before the brutal mob. "Behold I bring Him forth to you," he says (in a tone that seems to make amends), "that you may know that I find no cause in Him."

So Jesus came forth; and we may well imagine the yell of laughter and mockery that greeted His coming. For the coarse-minded soldiers had clothed Him in a purple garment, put a crown of thorns on His Head, and a cane in His Hands, as mock King of the Jews. "Behold," exclaims Pilate, "behold the Man!" Now indeed, he thought, they must be satisfied. Look at that faint, bleeding, anguish-spent Figure of the Son of Man, tricked out in those humbling trappings of mock royalty, and see, oh ye hard-hearted Jews, if He be longer an object of envy, scorn, or wrath; and not rather a sight to melt the very stones with pity and compassion! Then—then, the mob sways and surges like the ocean, and "Away!" is the fierce, brutal cry, "Away with Him! Crucify, crucify Him!"— The bloodthirsty miscreants! "Take Him you and crucify Him," he answers, out of very grief and vexation, "for I find no cause in Him." But he knew well enough they could do nothing of the kind. It rested with him to say the word; and would he

THE CALL OF PILATE.

say it?—"We have a law," is the surly rejoinder from the crowd—"we have a law, and according to that law He ought to die, because He made Himself the Son of God."[1]

"*He made Himself the Son of God!*" what manner of saying was this? The charge was new to Pilate. Jesus had been brought before him on the counts of treason and sedition—but Son of God! And then his wife's dream—what vision of evil-boding had the woman seen? Into what strange, unheard-of abyss of crime was he about to plunge? A Son of God! As a Roman, Pilate had been taught to believe that there were gods, and many. He would have heard or read, in the legends of his country, that gods had, sometime, walked the earth in the disguise of men! And then the meek, winning behaviour of the King of Truth, as He had styled Himself; His sweet, solemn tone; His truly royal bearing; the inward glory that shone in His mien and aspect! A Son of God—was He not worthy? All these thoughts would rush upon Pilate with a nameless horror. Fearful he was before; but "when Pilate therefore heard this saying," we read, "he feared the more; and he entered into the Hall again (whither Jesus had been led back), and he said to Jesus: (Oh, my brethren, mark well the fearful import of the question!) '*Whence art Thou?*' But Jesus gave him no answer."[2] And so, in that dread silence, came, for the third and last time, the Call of Grace: and for the third and last time also, surely, has Pilate told himself that he

[1] John xix. 4-7. [2] Ibid., vers. 8, 9.

will never, never do this sin which they ask him to commit.

Jesus was silent: wherefore? The question was to the purpose when the charge was of blasphemy; and he had answered it. When the High Priest had said: "I adjure Thee by the Living God that Thou tell us if Thou be the Christ, the Son of God," He had answered, in plain, awful words, "Thou hast said it;"[1] but the question was not to the purpose when the charge was, not of blasphemy, but of treason and sedition. That is true: but surely there is a better reason to be given why Jesus is silent now. There is a silence which is more eloquent than words. He had been asked to say the awful truth, if He were God from Heaven, or dust and ashes, like His questioner; and, in such a cause, to be silent was to affirm. And besides, the silence was merciful. Pilate has had light enough, if he will only use it. Let him think a little. Had not Jesus said that His Kingdom was not of this world? Well then, it was like King like Kingdom: the King was whence His Kingdom was. But oh, if he be going to abuse it, better far that he sin against less light, so he may still, in some sort, fall within scope of the prayer, "Father, forgive them, for they know not what they do."

At length Pilate himself breaks the silence: "Speakest Thou not to me? Knowest Thou not that I have power to crucify Thee, and I have power to release Thee?" "Thou shouldst not have any

---

[1] Matt. xxvi. 63, 64.

power against Me, unless it were given thee from above," is the answer. "Therefore, he that hath delivered Me to thee hath the greater sin."[1]

But why prolong the story to the world-known consummation? "From henceforth," continues the sacred narrative, "Pilate strove to release Him;" but only *strove*, whereas the power, he had just said, was in his hands. But he feared to use it; he was secretly in the power of the Jews, and dreaded lest an appeal to Rome might effect his removal from office in ruin and disgrace. And so he only strove. He had tried remonstrance; he had tried argument; he had appealed to their sense of justice, to their very pity; and now lastly he assumes a tone of levity and banter: "Behold *your King!*" he says; "shall I *crucify* your *King?*" But they only answer his grim jest in cruel earnest: "Away with Him! Crucify Him!" and, "If thou release this Man thou art not Cæsar's friend." "We have no king but Cæsar."[2] At this one word Pilate was vanquished; and so he said the word at last that he had thrice told his heart that he would never say. And the Cross was made ready, but for WHOM? Oh, what had He done! "Whence art Thou?" he had asked; but "Jesus gave him no answer."

This terrible question Pilate will ask himself until his dying day. There was one who had the greater sin, but oh, exceeding great was the sin of Pilate, and that he knew full well. For ever shall he see before the eyes of his soul the dread Victim of his sin, and

[1] John xix. 10, 11.   [2] Ibid., vers. 12, 14, 15.

that Victim his Maker and his Judge! "Behold the Man!" And then he will cry in the agony of his remorse, "I did it not, I never did it! Torment me not, sweet Saviour. It was the Jews, the cruel Jews, not I, that crucified Thee: lo! I wash my hands.—Ah, why does the Blood still cleave to them!" Oh, fruitless remorse! Oh, irrecoverable word! Oh, golden moments of mercy and grace, gone—gone, and never to be recalled!

How, you may ask me, brethren, does the history of this fearful crime concern ourselves? An awful interest belongs to the reading of it, but hardly a personal one. The rejection of so great a grace, the commission of so deadly a sin cannot have fallen to our lot. Enough for us to recall, during this solemn season, the sufferings and death of our crucified Redeemer; but hardly have we sinned like Pilate and the Jews. No? Have we never imitated, not indeed the enormity, but the manner of their sin? What cause then was it which brought down Jesus Christ from Heaven, to suffer and die, but our sins, and those of the whole world? Pilate, and the Jews, were indeed the instruments of His death; but they should have had no power against Him, unless it had been given them from above, and for our sakes.

Pilate had his hour of grace; but it passed him by, and left him with blood-stained hands. A moment Jesus stood before his face, and spoke within his soul; and he knew, or should have known, that it was God who spoke, and pleaded so powerfully with him, and within him; but he tampered with his conscience, as also we tamper with our conscience; not indeed in a matter of such awful moment, but still in matters of spiritual life and death. And Jesus Christ has looked upon us too, and called, and visited us, in the person of His minister in the sacred Tribunal of Penance, in the Holy Sacrament of the Altar; and in those hidden visitations of His grace, the secret of which is with our own heart. And gladly would we have hearkened to His Voice, but for those other voices which clamoured within our breast: Away with Him! away with Him for the lust of gold, away with Him for the lust of the flesh, away with Him for the lust of drink, away with Him for the Cæsar of this world, and its human respects; away with Him for self in every shape, and selfish passion and indulgence.

And then, to stifle the pangs of remorse, we speak words of sooth to our wounded souls, and thus wash we our hands—"I have never done anybody any harm. It is true I have been very neglectful of my religion; but there are plenty worse than I. I may fly in a passion and curse, now and then, but I am honest and sober; and I do not squander my substance, as so many others do;" or else, "I give into drink now and again, but I am not passionate like some, nor do I blaspheme in my drink, as others do; and I bear no malice against anybody;" or, "I know I have been very foolish and wicked, for I am a man of headstrong passions; but I am not bad-hearted, and I would not do a mean or base action for the world. I trust that the Lord will forgive me my sins; and I hope to set all right, one of these days." I, in short, am guiltless of this innocent Blood! let others look to it.

Oh, how deceitful is the heart of man, when it suffices for his justification that he has not sinned where he has not been tempted, and that he has always reverenced, in his heart, that divine law which he has violated in his deeds. But will God hold us guiltless of that Blood which Jesus Christ has shed on account of those very sins for which we now so lamely excuse ourselves? Oh, then, let us repent ourselves betimes, and beware how we crucify afresh the Son of God in our sins. So shall that precious Blood not for us indeed be shed in vain. So shall it cry to Heaven, no longer for vengeance against us, but for mercy and pardon. So shall it wash away our sinful stains, and blot out the handwriting that stands against us.

VII.

THE PENITENT THIEF.

"Remember me, Lord, when Thou shalt come into Thy Kingdom."
—LUKE xxiii. 39.

THERE can hardly be a more foolish delusion than that wherein sinners flatter themselves in their wicked courses, that they will at some future time or other—at least on their death-bed—amend their state, and be converted to God. For Almighty God, who gives to us the present acceptable time, has not promised us a future wherein to repent. But to pass over this and other such-like considerations, I wish rather to ask only this one question:—

Is there any good reason to think that it will be easier to be converted, at the last, than it is *now?* For consider what conversion is. It is the change of heart towards God, of one who had turned away from Him to love some creature or other better than God; so far better than God, as to be willing grievously to offend Him, rather than forego the pleasure of this guilty love. And so the question finally comes to this: Will the man who cannot love God now, yet easily change to love Him, on his death-bed? He who loves the thought of sinful pleasures now, will he hate the thought of sinful pleasures then? He who loves money better than God now, will he love God better than money then? He who cannot forbear to entertain a guilty image now, will he loathe such guilty image then? He who is not in earnest now (and the man who postpones his conversion is convicted by the very fact of want of earnestness), will he be in earnest then? Now does this sound reasonable? Is it likely? Does it agree with what we know of our own hearts? And, on the other hand, is it not the fact, that, as a rule, men die as they have lived?

But you will say: oh, but death is a great disenchanter! When this world, and all those vain creatures which, in our blind folly, we have chosen before God, begin to fade away from before our dying eyes, then indeed we shall know, however late, both His infinite value and their empty nothingness. And then, we know that, in whatsoever hour the sinful man shall turn away from his wickedness,—though it be at the very last breath of his life,—that in that same hour, in that very moment, God will surely turn to him, and accept his tardy repentance! —Yes, my brethren, the thought of death is indeed a saving thought: and if it move us *now*, surely it will move us then, and with power. But how if it move us not at all now? in that case will it move us then? I think it might frighten us; but is a repentance, *through fright*, likely to be sincere? And then, many sinners are not even frightened at their death. They had not the fear of God in health; so neither were they moved by it in their last sickness. That is natural enough. For a man does not change his character by dying, except in the same manner that he may change it in living.

Now Holy Scripture furnishes us with an instance of one who repented through fright, in his last moments; but his repentance was not accepted. The wicked King, Antiochus, when, in punishment of his many cruelties and sacrileges, he was smitten with an ulcerous disease, which rendered him unbearable alike to his attendants and to himself, exclaimed, "It is just, to be subject to God, and that a mortal man should not equal himself with God. Then," we read, "this wicked man prayed to the Lord, *of Whom he was not to obtain mercy.*"[1]

No, my brethren, the great difficulty with the practised sinner is to change the heart; and such change is, at least, just as difficult in sickness as in health. And this being the case, so far from taking their final acceptance as a thing of course, we should rather wonder that such persons do not fall into downright despair of their salvation; and indeed it would be only natural for them to do so, except for one grand consideration; and that is the wonder-working power of the grace of God, which is given to all who ask it of Him in sincerity and earnestness. For the change of heart, which conversion implies, is

[1] 2 Machab. ix. 12, 13.

not in the power of man, without God: it must be the work of the Right-hand of the Most High. This is the lesson which the Good Thief preaches to us from his cross, and which I ask you this morning, to meditate with me, brethren. I do not think that his example, fully considered, is such as to tempt any one to presume; but at any rate, it teaches that none are so miserable that they need despair.

For surely nothing can be more wonderful than this conversion. The man was a robber, had led the life of a robber, and had some of the worst of a robber's crimes upon his soul, since he owned to his hardened comrade that he did not think even the death of the cross a worse punishment than his sins had deserved: "We receive the due reward of our deeds," he said, "but this man hath done no evil."[1] It is rare indeed to find a penitent out of men of his class.

It would appear that, until the sweet moment when the grace of Jesus found him, he was no better than his reprobate companion; for, we read that "they who were crucified with Him, reviled Him."[2] Perhaps this might be only a fashion of speaking; for men sometimes say "*they*" when only one person is intended. But indeed it is only too likely that he blasphemed at the first. He would, probably, never before have seen our Blessed Saviour, until they met on the way to Calvary. But he soon learnt, from the shouts of the rabble, what the real offence, in their eyes, of Jesus was, that "He made Himself the Son

---

[1] Luke xxiii. 41. [2] Mark xv. 32.

of God;" and this awful, saving truth would sound, in his rude, carnal ears, like a sorry jest. And so, while he writhed and cursed, robber-like, under that hideous nailing (for he *was* nailed: maybe, he was bound with cords, as the pictures show; but if so he was nailed as well; it was the custom)—while he was nailed, I say; while he hung upon his cross in torments unendurable, what wonder if, like his brutal comrade, he found, even in the meek, suffering Jesus, an object whereon to vent some of the deadly spite and rage that filled his heart. "He saved others," cried the priests and the scribes, " Himself he cannot save. If He be the King of Israel, let Him now come down from the cross, and we will believe in Him. He trusted in God; let Him now deliver Him . . . for He said, 'I am the Son of God.' And the selfsame thing the thieves also, who were crucified together with Him, reproached Him with."[1]

But, sooner or later, there was a change; for he has begun to scan the sacred Person of Jesus with a closer scrutiny. In spite of the unspeakable tortures which he endures, he has his wits about him; for the cross, while it racked the members, left the brain free, and the senses wakeful. He watches Jesus then; and would note, with ever-growing wonder, how unlike human sufferer is He whom they had styled in scorn the King of the Jews. How meekly He had laid Him down upon His Cross, as on a bed, and yielded dumbly His tender Hands and Feet to the nailing! And then, when the Cross was

[1] Matt. xxvii. 41, *et seq.*

upreared, and the fire of torment, he knew well, must have been at fever-heat, this One had uttered nor word, nor groan of complaint; or, if He spoke at all, it was only to pray for the very men who so ruthlessly tortured—for the very men who, like himself, had just now cursed and reviled Him: "Father," He had said, "forgive them, for they know not what they do!"

He had called God *His Father:* yes, this was the *real cause* (not the treason and sedition for which Pilate had condemned Him) for which He suffered. "He made Himself the Son of God" (the mob would not let Him forget that for a single moment), He had said that He was the Son of God, and Saviour of the world. How now, if this word, at which he had just now scoffed, as at the raving of a maniac—how if it were *true?* How, if He were indeed the Son of God, and promised Saviour? Saviour! oh, welcome word, if this were so, in his hour of bitterest need! Who wanted a Saviour as he wanted, on this, oh, utterly unendurable cross? His sins had found him out indeed; and yet, though terrible the punishment, he owned aloud that that punishment was just. And while men had sent him to the cross, for crimes committed against them, he was about to fall (awful thought!) into the hands of the living God! Alas, alas! was he to lose at once both this world and the next? Was there no hope, even for such a wretch as himself? Mercy from man there was none: could he hope to find it with God, Whom he had ever outraged in his wild, lawless life? And—for he must have thought it; it is only natural—would it not be a downright mockery of God, to turn to Him now, just because there was no other resource? Oh, what words can paint the wretched plight of this man, in body and soul! Already he writhes in a hell of torments on his cross, from which even death itself would be a sweet relief, but for that terrible after-death, when God's judgment would begin!

And so, when the scornful cry rose up again from the mob, of a Saviour Who could not save, and was taken up by his comrade, he rebuked him; for the torment had broken the poor fellow's spirit; the sweet work of grace had begun in him, and he had humbled himself under the chastening hand of God: "Neither dost thou fear God," he said, "seeing that thou art under the same condemnation; and we indeed justly, for we receive the due reward of our deeds; but this man hath done no evil." And then he turns a tearful, longing eye on his Saviour, and, "Lord," he says, "remember me, when Thou shalt come into Thy Kingdom!" And, oh, joy of joys (more than he had dared to ask, or dreamed of asking), he receives from the lips of Jesus the assurance of immediate salvation. "Amen, I say unto thee, this day thou shalt be with Me in Paradise."[1] And so he passed into his rest, the first-fruits of the redemption of Calvary.

Such was the wonderful conversion of the Good Thief, as he is called. And I have tried to fancy, and describe it, as indeed it may have really happened,

[1] Luke xxiii. 41–43.

by way of showing you, brethren, that such a conversion, on the point of death, is nothing different *in kind*, however wonderful it be, from the conversions of those whose lives are spared to them. They who think that, as a matter of course, they will repent at the hour of death, have to account how it was that that other robber, who had, so to speak, just the same chances, did not also repent. What was it then that made the awful difference between these two sinners, that the one was saved, and the other (humanly speaking) lost? The same that makes the difference between men who are not dying. The call of God seeks out each man in his turn, and one is taken and the other left. The hand of God is laid on them in affliction, and one is chastened and humbled, while another is only hardened all the more in his heart of pride and selfishness. The visible judgments of God, His wondrous testimonies and miracles, and the signs of the times and the day of visitation, are manifest to all; but they are unheeded, or misread, save by the simple and the humble and earnest. And while one man does not own the Lord of Glory, though He have come in power into His Kingdom; another finds his Saviour even on the malefactor's gibbet, and becomes a disciple at the very moment when their Lord has become a scandal, even to disciples.

Wonderful conversion truly! but, after all, it only goes to show that a man may be converted at any moment, *if he only will.* He may repent in earnest, even on his death-bed, like the Good Thief, and like him be accepted. I only say that there is no hope or likelihood that he will do so, if he is never in earnest now, when the opportunity is offered.

For, my brethren, I come back to the thought with which I started: I can never believe that a man whom nothing can induce to repentance now, will repent at the last, merely because he happens to be dying. And if the thief on his cross, by a singular grace of God, turned to his Redeemer and was saved, I am only led to think that such a grace, had it found him living, instead of dying, would equally have effected his conversion. But God does not give such singular graces to all His creatures, though He gives to all men graces abundantly sufficient for their salvation. The case of this thief's conversion is a very exceptional case. We can argue nothing from exceptional cases: what is the rule? Inquire of pastors, who have experience of the sick-bed, and they will tell you that the vast number of those who have been seemingly converted on the prospect of death, when contrary to expectation they have been restored to health, have reverted to their former course of life. So it comes at last to the old, well-worn axiom, that the only preparation for a good death is a good life. And hence it is written: "He that hurteth, let him hurt still; and he that is filthy, let him be filthy still; and he that is just, let him be justified still; and he that is holy, let him be sanctified still. Behold, I come quickly: and my reward is with Me, *to render to every man according to his works.*"[1]

[1] Apoc. xxii. 11, 12.

And St. Paul warns us to the same effect, that "God is *not mocked*. For what things a man shall sow, those also shall he reap. For he that soweth in his flesh, of the flesh shall reap corruption; but he that soweth in the spirit, of the spirit shall reap life everlasting."[1] And again we are admonished in Holy Scripture not to defer the work of salvation until the morrow, but, "To-day if ye shall hear His Voice, harden not your hearts:"[2] for there is no to-morrow for the sinner; it must be *now*, when God calls, or never.

They who trifle with the matter of salvation, can find, at any rate, no encouragement from the example of the Penitent Thief. If we had read of him that he was of the number of those who propose to themselves to lead a wicked life, and to avoid its consequences by a repentant death, then indeed the gospel might well have spared his history. But it is only said of him that he had sinned, and that he repented, though at the very last moment of the eleventh hour; and that he was saved, yet so as by the fire of the torments of Calvary. His example bids the most wretched hope; but, as I have said, it warrants none in presumption.

[1] Gal. vi. 7, 8.   [2] Ps. xciv. 8.

VIII.

THE TEMPTATION OF THE CROSS.

"For we have not a High Priest who cannot have compassion on our infirmities, but One tempted in all things like as we are, without sin."—HEB. iv. 15.

THE word temptation is frequently used in Holy Scripture in the meaning of tribulation or affliction; as when our Lord speaks of His Apostles as "having continued with Him in His *temptations*,"[1] *i.e.*, trials and troubles; or St. James bids the faithful to "count it all joy when they shall fall into divers *temptations*."[2] And in this sense, surely, St. Paul speaks of Christ in the text, as being tempted like ourselves; for what infirmity was in our Lord, the experience of which enabled Him to compassionate our own, but the griefs and torments which He sustained for our sakes; since other infirmity He knew none? In these then He was "tempted like as we are, in all things, without sin:" as also another text of the same Apostle confirms, which says that Christ, "wherein He Himself hath suffered, and been

---

[1] Luke xxii. 28. [2] James i. 2.

tempted, is able to succour also them that are tempted."[1] I shall therefore enlarge on this view of the case in speaking, as the present season demands, on the sacred Passion of our divine Redeemer; because I think it will appear not only that suffering was in an especial manner His temptation, but that herein was the very respect in which His trial resembled our own, and in which, though sinless by nature, He was able to serve as a model in the probation of sinful creatures like ourselves.

For in one sense it is obvious that our Blessed Saviour could not have been tempted like ourselves; because in Him there was not that wretched sympathy with what is sinful, which is in ourselves as the consequence of Adam's transgression, and is what makes temptation, in our case, so perilous; but He could be tempted like ourselves, in the respect that temptation itself is a kind of *suffering*, from which we too often seek relief in sinning; which we speak of as the *force* of temptation, and plead in excuse for our sins. This force of temptation our Blessed Lord knew, from the very nature of His trial, as none but Himself could ever have known it: it is simply the trouble that arises in us from the restraint of self-denial; and who ever denied himself as He did? He knew what it was to crave for bread, as in the wilderness, when He must not have it; to toil and sweat, when He might have been in ease and comfort; to wander

[1] Heb. ii. 18.

like an outcast, "having not where to lay His Head," when He might have been well housed and at rest: or, to sum up all in the words of the Apostle, "Christ *pleased not* Himself;"[1] but, "having joy set before Him, endured the Cross,"[2] in obedience to the Will of His heavenly Father.

In this sense, then, which is that of my text, and carries me beyond what is commonly known as the Temptation of Christ, His whole life, but especially, which I am to consider, His sacred Passion, was His temptation. In treating on the matter from this point of view, I propose to dwell chiefly on two main features in our Blessed Saviour's trial, which, I think, must have unspeakably aggravated it, viz., in the first place, that it was *foreseen;* and, in the next place, that it was *voluntary.*

1. Perhaps some amongst you may remember to have seen a print, in which our Lord is depicted, as a boy, engaged in the occupation of His foster-father, St. Joseph. The divine Child is arrested in His work, and a shadow has fallen on His brow; for the wood beneath His hands appears to have taken the form of a *cross.* The incident, though a mere devout fancy of the artist, is true to the *spirit* of the gospel narrative. From the first, the shadow of the Cross was on the life of Jesus. What we are to suffer, in life or death, is mercifully hidden from us; and though the prospect be never so gloomy, it is only natural in us to hope for the best; but for our Blessed Saviour there was no such hope. To Him,

[1] Rom. xv. 3.   [2] Heb. xii. 2.

the curtain which veils the Future was always uplifted, and His whole life in its every circumstance, with its bitter consummation, was ever before the mind's eye. While His hour was not yet come, He distinctly foreknew that it *would* come, the when and how, its every token: "Go and tell that fox," He said, when told that Herod sought His life, "Behold I cast out devils, and do cures to-day and to-morrow, and the third day I am consummated; nevertheless, I must walk to-day and to-morrow and the day following; because it cannot be that a prophet perish out of Jerusalem."[1] True, that the Cross is not inscribed on every page of our Lord's life; it is not even so frequent a topic of His sacred discourse as one might have expected; so that it came as a surprise to the disciples going to Emmaus, that "the Christ was to suffer, and so enter into His glory." As some great hero of this world does not betray, at all times and seasons, the lofty purpose that shapes his life; but he is engaged, distracted, interested, and diverted in divers ways; yet the purpose is always *there:* it is all the more real, because it lies in the depths and not on the mere changing surface of the soul: so with our Blessed Saviour: He attends the marriage-feast; He is a guest at Simon's, or at Levi's banquet; He teaches and preaches; He blesses the children; He is exercised in deeds of benevolence. Save when retired a space in prayer, or in the lonely vigils of the night, He is always occupied, in one way or

---

[1] Luke xiii. 32, 33.

another; as if to teach us by His example, that work, as well as prayer, is a remedy for heart griefs and temptations. But, alas! He can never quite forget the cross, which is the sacred purpose of His life. And though He would not, as men are often wont to do, make parade of His griefs, as though He leant on human sympathy, yet, on the other hand, He would not wholly avoid it, for our instruction. So once, it would seem, He suddenly breaks the thread of His discourse, and exclaims: "I am come to cast fire upon the earth; and what will I, but that it be kindled? And I have a baptism wherewith I am to be baptized, and how am I straitened till it be accomplished!"[1] But there was another and very notable occasion, when He vouchsafed to reveal to us, that what He afterwards suffered in the garden of Gethsemane, was, in some measure, the trial of His whole life. It was when His hour drew nigh, that certain strangers who had come up into Jerusalem for the festival, sought, through Philip, an interview with His divine Master: "Sir," they said, "we would see Jesus." Whereupon, "Philip cometh and telleth Andrew. Again, Andrew and Philip told Jesus." When our Blessed Lord, it seems to me, acted in a manner unlike Himself; for when they are introduced, He speaks like one pre-occupied with His own thought, and rather thinking aloud than addressing themselves, though He spoke to them: "And Jesus answered them, saying: 'The hour is come that the Son of Man should be glorified.

---

[1] Luke xii. 49, 50.

Amen, amen, I say to you, unless the grain of wheat fall into the ground, and die, itself abideth alone; but if it die, it bringeth forth much fruit.'" Then the thought of His death upon the cross induces with it all the bitter anguish, and, "Now," He exclaims, "is My soul troubled, and what shall I say? Father, save Me from this hour!—but for this cause came I unto this hour."[1] He was not weak, for He was strong in His love; but He would seem weak, that He might show us He "knew what was in man," and what it was to be tempted. As if He could no longer endure it, but *must* speak; and because, as the former text explains, He is *straitened*, that is, urged contrariwise; the Will of His heavenly Father, His own divine charity compelling Him one way, and the natural repugnance of torment to flesh and blood constraining Him, on the other. In a sense, He wills, and not wills: is not such *straitness* the very essence of temptation, in which excess of pain or passion seems as if it would suffocate the very freedom of the soul?

And observe, brethren, that our Blessed Saviour's trial was, in one sense, all the greater, while the dread hour was only yet in apprehension. Have you never known what it is to expect some blow to fall, which, you know, *must* fall, and it tarries? Better, far better, you have thought, to suffer at once, while the nerves are braced for suffering, than endure this protracted torment of delay, in which one suffers an agony multiplied at every moment. True, that, in

[1] John xii. 21-25, 27.

our case, suspense exaggerates such torment: we want to know, and at once, the very worst; whereas, in our divine Saviour, this suspense, in which fancy shapes horrors for itself, could have no place: but, alas! was it any mitigation of the grief of Jesus that He always knew the worst; that He must perforce, in prospect, die His death a thousand times —and such a death as, if we realised it as it was, we could hardly endure to think about? The temptation reached its climax in the garden of Gethsemane, when it overmastered in Him, as temptation can overmaster in ourselves, everything except *the will.* His hour was come; He saw it as He had ever seen it; but He sees it now, no longer as in the future; for it is at hand: it is now, presently. It is at hand, and yet it tarries; like the slow night of the sick-bed, when it seems to the poor sufferer time itself is choked; and each moment, big with its own agony, an ever-enduring now. It is at hand, and yet it tarries; while there is time to taste of every ingredient in the bitter cup, as He only could have tasted, Who not only foreboded, but *foreknew.* It is at hand, and yet it tarries; while His divine Mind, like the clearest mirror, showed Him, not shadows or phantoms, but realities. He sees, plain as eyesight could show; nay, He feels, and hears too, in a sense, all that will just now be. Already, in the spirit, He is in the hands of the rabble; He reads their brutal looks; His ears ring with their yells; His limbs ache with their cords; He is dragged, and haled, and hustled about; they smite His cheeks, and pluck Him by the beard, and spit in His sacred Face. Anon, He writhes in the red agony of the scourge; He is mocked with the purple rag, and cane sceptre, and crown of thorns: and, at last, half blind, and spent with anguish, they nail Him to the wood; and He is lifted up in the air, hanging, partly by His own gaping wounds, in the horrors of such a death as, if I should be able, I could not bear to tell, or you to hear it.

Nor indeed am I, at present, so much concerned to describe the awful sufferings of our Blessed Saviour, as to consider them in the light of the text, and as they mainly constituted His temptation. The dread prospect of the Cross, then, I say, was enough, in itself, to crush the spirit of Jesus; but ah, there was added the still worse heart-ache over the sinfulness and thanklessness of men, in whose behalf He was to undergo it all; and the double torment, it seemed, was unendurable; "He began to fear," we read, "and to be heavy:" His grief was like to kill Him; for His soul, He complained to His disciples, "was sorrowful, even unto death." Nay, He already agonised; and His death-sweat fell upon the ground "as drops of blood." The prayer which He then made to His heavenly Father reveals, in a few words, how terrible, to the human soul of Jesus, was the Temptation of the Cross: "Father, if it be possible, let this chalice pass from Me: nevertheless, not as I will, but as Thou wilt!" *If it were possible*—ah, here is the sting of the agony—here the very knot of the temptation! He knew only too well, that *one*.

way, it was indeed possible: it simply rested with Himself, if the sinful race of men should ever see the salvation of God. He was now, as ever, free to suffer or not; but if the world was to be saved, He knew what, in His Father's Will, was to be the awful price!

2. And thus I am led to consider that other feature in the trial of our Blessed Saviour, that it was voluntary. We know little indeed of the sacred Passion of Christ, if we have not understood what, in one shape or another, is so frequently inculcated in the Holy Scriptures, that the Sacrifice was, on His part, a pure free-will offering. "He was offered," says the Prophet, "because it was His own will; and He opened not His mouth."[1] "When He cometh into the world, He saith: Sacrifice and oblation Thou wouldest not; but a body Thou hast fitted for Me: holocausts for sin did not please Thee: then, said I, Behold I come! In the head of the Book it is written of Me, that I should do Thy Will, O God."[2] But indeed it is needless to cite texts of Scripture in support of a statement which is plain enough, in the very nature of the case; that, neither as God, nor as Man, was Jesus bound to suffer the awful agony of the Cross—or suffer aught at all. For what had He done, the meek and gentle Lamb of God, that He should be doomed to death? or what was man, that He should be compelled to be mindful of him at so lavish a price? He was not doomed: He doomed Himself. It was His Father's Will; but

[1] Isaias liii. 7.   [2] Heb. x. 5-7.

it was not, strictly speaking, His Father's command. It was His Father's Will, if only He Himself would comply. Once, indeed, He speaks of it as a "commandment" which He had received of His Father, that He should lay down His life;[1] but *in itself* it was not so. It was His own love that gave it all the force, and made it stand to Him in the stead of a commandment. His Father's Will was law, because He held it as such; and to do it, He had said, was His "meat and drink." He had ever chosen it with His human will; He chose it now. He could be tempted; but He could not waver. He the divine Hero, the Holy One of God—He could not act as less divinely noble than Himself; He could not, through His own default, make void the sweet heavenly scheme of mercy and salvation to men which He had come into the world to execute: He could not spoil the lofty purpose of His life—though, in a very real sense, He was free to do so. The Good Shepherd, since it must needs be so, would lay down His life for His sheep. But not the less sharp was the Cross, because He freely chose it; not the less sore the temptation, because He well knew that He would never consent to it.

On the contrary, the fire of torment was only all the more provoked because it was voluntary. Worse is the craving of hunger or thirst, if bread is to be had, but one must not eat; water within reach, but one must not drink. A man sometimes must have his limbs restrained by force, who suffers under

[1] John x. 18.

THE TEMPTATION OF THE CROSS.

the surgeon's knife, though he freely consents to the operation. Which of us could hold a red-hot iron in his hand, for only a few moments, even to save his life? On the other hand, men often evince the greatest fortitude and patience in enduring the pains of sickness; for the simple reason that they cannot avoid it. The thought that their own will has just nothing to do with the matter, and that they will have to bear it all the same, whether they submit or rebel against it, acts as a support. But our Blessed Saviour, I repeat, was at each and every moment free to suffer or not, to live or die; just as free as ourselves, when we are tempted, but prefer the holy Will of God to our own pleasure, or profit. He exulted in the thought that His life was in His own Hand. "Therefore doth the Father love Me," He had said, "because I lay down My life, that I may take it again. No man taketh it from Me; but I lay it down of Myself; and I have power to lay it down, and I have power to take it up again."[1] To save it, if He would have saved it, He could have asked the Father, and He would have "given Him presently more than twelve legions of angels." But indeed there was no need; for when that band came, armed with clubs and staves to apprehend Him, at His very word, that "I am He," "they went backward, and fell to the ground." Thus He showed His power, for the first time and the last. It was enough to have shown it. He needed not to speak one word, to raise a finger; He had only to shape a

[1] John x. 18.

will to that intent, and in a moment the anguish of Gethsemane had been changed for the glory of Thabor; the knotted scourge had foregone its smart; their hands had withered that hammered in the nails; or He had burst those iron bonds asunder, come down from the cross, and passed unharmed from out their midst, as it had been before. But, alas, it cannot, must not be so now! And so, instead, He falls in anguish on His Face, and like the weakest man amongst us, prays the Father for help to endure that which, to unaided human strength, is unendurable. Well might He bid His disciples "watch and pray lest ye enter into temptation," who was thus made Himself, not only to know (He knew it) but to *feel* what was temptation. What man was ever tempted in pleasure, as the Son of God was tempted in pain?

And ah, there was One at hand who knew only too well how to add to all the bitter horror of the trial! We read that when that temptation in the desert was finished, "the devil left Him," and it is significantly added *"for a time."*[1] He came back, then, oftentimes no doubt: he would surely come now; our Blessed Lord had said as much: the Prince of Darkness would not be absent in his own hour of the "power of darkness."[2] In the garden, amidst the rabble, in the Hall of Judgment, amongst the soldiers, at the Cross he would whisper close, as each occasion served, with fresh effect, the old suggestion, "*If Thou be the Son of God,*"—— all the

---

[1] Luke iv. 13. [2] Ibid. xxii. 53.

more cruel, on that account, because it could never prevail. He would probe Him to the quick, if He were Son of God, or no. He would tempt, and if temptation could nought avail, why then in baffled rage he would torment: such is his double office. "If He were the Son of God, why then was it *thus*, and *thus*? Let Him, at least, have some compassion on Himself: what *man* could suffer more? The very prospect of the agony had been itself an agony; how then should He bear the event? The scourge was fierce, but fiercer far the Cross! Death, in any shape indeed, was terrible—but such a death as this unendurable, horrible, detestable! it would not bear thinking about." Then, still and ever at fault, the wily Fiend would change, in a moment, the front of the temptation, and vent his sudden spite: "If He were the Son of God—but no: the torture had found Him out, had unmasked Him what He was. That searching lash had fetched into His eyes most human tears that asked the beholders' pity; because, in good sooth, He could neither endure it, nor help Himself. The Son of God! where then were His Father's thunderbolts, the while men smote His Face, and plucked His beard, and spit upon Him— the vilest outrage! Nor could He so much as tell the name of him who smote and outraged Him: no, nor so much as bid but a wind of heaven to fan His fevered brow, nor show others the smallest token of divinity; but He was wholly in the hands of men who worked their will upon Him, and nailed Him to the wood. The Son of God! what, *crucified between two thieves!*" And a hundred voices echoed the Tempter's words: "He made Himself to be the Son of God," they would tell one another; it had been put to the test, and had ended thus. "He trusted in God;" said the priests and the scribes, "let Him now deliver Him, if he will have Him; for He said, 'I am the Son of God;'" and "Let Christ, the King of Israel, now come down from the Cross, that we may see and believe!" "If Thou be the Son of God, save Thyself and us," urged the graceless thief. Yes, "Save Thine own Self," shouted the rabble. "If Thou be the Son of God, come down from the Cross."[1]

Cruel words! and in most cruel season were they spoken, when Jesus, in His sore afflicted human nature, seemed to Himself indeed as He were less than God. For it was the sad hour of His dereliction, the utmost acme of temptation, and fiercest extreme of mortal anguish. How shall I say it? In His utmost need, in the very excess of the death-agony, that craves the help of God, His own divine Hand (for he was, throughout all, his own Doomster) shut off from Himself all the flood-gates of heavenly consolation; and a sheer human voice complains: "My God, my God, why hast Thou forsaken Me?" So, if any wretch, living or dying, should ever suffer some image of an agony like this, which seems as it would blacken Heaven itself, and blot out to him almost the very Face of God, let him remember, even so, that "the disciple is not greater than his Master;"

[1] Matt. xxvii. 40-43; Mark xv. 32.

and Jesus suffered that before. Enough: it is the last fell drop in the Cup of Calvary; but it *is* the last, and the voice of the Man of Sorrows is followed by the Voice of God confest. For Jesus passed away with a mighty cry, that made the centurion beat his breast in fear, and exclaim that He "was indeed the Son of God:" "Jesus, crying out with a loud voice, gave up the ghost." What means this loud voice, my brethren? What does He say, God's Holy One? Ah, it is the shout of Victory: "It is consummated!" the conflict is done and finished: He has fought and He has won for Himself, and for all of us who shall fight in His Name till time itself is run out!

And thus was our Blessed Saviour "tempted, like as we are, in all things without sin," and passed through the furnace of tribulation into the glory which He had with the Father before the world was made. The sacred Passion of our Divine Saviour has many lessons for us; let this one suffice for the present, that Jesus is our model and our comfort in the warfare with the enemies of our salvation. What better motive to cover us with confusion for the past, to inspire us with ardour and fortitude for the future, to inflame our hearts with divine charity, than this consideration of the Temptation of the Cross? When then we are faint and disheartened, because the Kingdom of Heaven suffers in us a little salutary violence; when, solicited by the soft blandishments of pleasure, we almost waver in our will; when beset with evil thoughts, which only therefore are bitter to us because we hate them, only therefore a torment because we know that, with God's help, we will never consent to them; when wearied with the importunity, or encompassed in the straitness of temptation, the Enemy shall suggest the fatal relief of sin, then let us lift up our eyes to Jesus upon the Cross, and He will be our consolation and our strength. When tempted, like Himself, no longer in pleasure, but in pain; when sickness or infirmity shall be our portion unto chastisement; when the terrors of death assail us, and the devil is come down against us in great wrath, "knowing that he hath but a short time;"[1] in that supreme hour of the power of darkness, we shall look upon Jesus in His agony, who therefore became partaker of our flesh and blood, "that, through death, He might destroy him that had the empire of death . . . and might deliver them who, through fear of death, were all their lifetime subject to servitude . . . for wherein He Himself hath suffered, and been tempted, He is able to succour them also that are tempted."[2]

[1] Apoc. xii. 12.   [2] Heb. ii. 14, 15, 18.

IX.

OUR BLESSED SAVIOUR'S RESURRECTION.

"Therefore, because the children are partakers of flesh and blood, He also Himself, in like manner, hath been partaker of the same; that, through death, He might destroy him who had the empire of death (that is to say, the devil), and might deliver them that, through fear of death, were all their lifetime subject to servitude."— HEB. ii. 14, 15.

THAT the Resurrection of our Blessed Saviour is the sovereign antidote to the fear of death is a lesson which we should have hardly cared to dwell upon, on Easter Sunday, because the very subject of death, associated as it is in our minds with every gloomy feeling, is one which seems incongruous with so essentially joyous a festival. That is natural enough, but after we have allowed full course to the tide of gladness which swells in the heart while we contemplate our newly-risen Lord in the radiance of His immortal human nature, it were well to consider, as I now propose to do, that the gospel of the Resurrection is, for this very reason, the gladdest tidings ever announced to men, because it has destroyed the sting of death, and shed a light of glory over the grave. So that in the very proportion that the thought of death is distasteful to us is our need of that remedy which was a chief object of the death and Resurrection of Christ; who, as the text declares, therefore assumed our human nature that He might die in it, and through His own death overthrow the empire of death, and so "deliver them that, through fear of death, were all their lifetime subject to servitude."

But a truth is only fruitful to us in the measure that we realise it; and it is impossible, from the nature of the case, that we should realise the fact of the Resurrection as they must have realised who had "seen and touched and handled of the Word of Life." And although they are pronounced blessed in the gospel, who, like ourselves, "have not seen, and have believed," yet are not such Christians called blessed, precisely because they have believed at a disadvantage? For certainly we are at a disadvantage, as compared with those who saw with their own eyes, unless we strive to compensate ourselves with such aids as are in our power. And to this end, brethren, I would have you to consider Christ risen, "the First-fruits of them that sleep,"[1] not merely as a doctrine, but as a fact. I wish you to listen to the story of the Resurrection, as recorded in the sacred Text, and to ponder with me all the wonder of it, as if (if this were possible) you were hearing it for the first time. So shall you be enabled all the more

[1] 1 Cor. xv. 20.

effectually to bring home its joyous lesson to the comfort of your hearts and souls.

Consider then, in the first place, what could be more strange, in itself, than that a man, whom, by every unmistakable token, one saw die, and dead, should suddenly appear amongst his friends alive and well, and behave and converse with them as before his death? As was indeed the case with Lazarus, whom, in one chapter of the gospel, we read of as dead and buried, and, in another, as alive again, and present at a banquet with his relatives; being raised out of the very grave at the word of his Saviour. I can fancy that a man who witnessed such a miracle would be so dazzled and distraught at the very wonder of it, that he would be almost persuaded to doubt the evidence of his senses, or would express himself, when questioned about it, in contradictory phrase, after the manner of him who said: "I believe; Lord, help my unbelief!" And, no doubt, the fact that Lazarus now lived would only have convinced many of the Jews that (however the matter had been secretly contrived) he was never truly dead: still, they who witnessed the miracle—who saw him surely die, and again saw him surely alive—must have believed; for in such a case the proverb holds, that "Seeing is believing." But then—when they saw the great Restorer Himself in the arms of death upon the Cross, with the sweat of death on His brow, and the hue of death on His cheek; when they heard the jeering cry, "He saved others, Himself He cannot save," which must have echoed the voice of many a failing heart; when He breathed, at length, in the manner they only breathe who never breathe again; when He was, in short, dead and buried—what then about the past? What of His wondrous Life? What of His miracles? If only the grave could hold Him, and the Father should "suffer His Holy One to see corruption," would not all be involved in this one, cold, dark doubt? As, on the other hand, His Resurrection would at once set the seal on all His other miracles. Hence, says St. Paul: "If Christ be not risen again, your faith is vain; for you are yet in your sins. Then, they also who are fallen asleep in Christ are perished. If, in this life only, we have hope in Christ, we are of all men most miserable."[1]

What a trial, then, to the faith of the disciples, must have been the death of their divine Master. Well might He warn them, saying: "All you shall be scandalised in Me this night. For it is written: 'I will strike the Shepherd, and the sheep of the flock shall be dispersed.'"[2] And yet, even in this very hour of trial and darkness, a convert is added to the Faith, and the thief exclaims from his cross: "Remember me, Lord, when Thou shalt come into Thy Kingdom!" It was a trial therefore which need not have been fatal to the belief of the disciples, yet a severe trial it was, and fatal where faith was weak. I shall dwell upon it, in order that we may apprehend all the more keenly, by way of contrast, the startling glory of the Resurrection, and that we

---

[1] 1 Cor. xv. 16, *et seq.*   [2] Matt. xxvi. 31.

may apprehend it, as I said before, not merely as a doctrine, but as a *fact*.

Upon the death of our Blessed Saviour on the Cross, then, faith in Him as the promised Redeemer was in the minds of many, at least, of the disciples, obscured or gone. "Our chief priests and princes delivered Him to be condemned to death, and crucified Him. But we hoped that it was He that should have redeemed Israel: and now, besides all this, to-day is the third day since these things were done,"[1]—such was the sad discourse held by the two disciples on the way to Emmaus. Nor were they by any means alone in their unbelief. For when Mary Magdalen told the disciples, "who were mourning and weeping,". that the Lord "was alive, and had been seen by her, they did not believe."[2] "Neither," when the two disciples to whom He had revealed Himself at Emmaus told the rest, "did they believe *them*."[3] And then there is the case of that Apostle whose unbelief has passed into a proverb, who said: "Except I shall see in His Hands the print of the nails, and put my finger into the place of the nails, and put my hand into His Side, I will not believe:"[4] a very human saying; and, as such, not commended by our Lord. They ought, as He had said, to have read to better purpose the Law and the Prophets, wherein it was written that the Christ was "to have suffered these things, and so to enter into His glory."[5] Nay they ought to have remembered, what did not

---

[1] Luke xxiv. 20. [2] Mark xvi. 10, 11. [3] Ibid. ver. 13.
[4] John xx. 25. [5] Luke xxiv. 26.

escape the memory even of His enemies, how He Himself had promised that He would arise: "Sir," the priests said to Pilate, "we have remembered that that seducer said, while He was yet alive: 'After three days, I will rise again;'"[1] but, in the hour of gloom and sorrow, men forget the hope of happier days.

The trial, else too hard to bear, was of short duration. First came the rumour of the holy women, who had visited the Sepulchre at early dawn, and told the disciples how "they found Him not, but had seen a vision of angels;" but "these words seemed to them as idle tales; and they did not believe them."[2] Then He manifested Himself to the two at Emmaus, and afterwards to the whole assembly of the disciples. Let us strive, brethren, to view the event with their eyes who saw, and have described it for us, and to enter into their feelings, as they passed from wondering doubt to conviction, certainty, knowledge.

First came that instinctive horror which ever accompanies an experience of the supernatural: "They (the disciples) being troubled and frighted, supposed that they saw a spirit;"[3] "They yet believed not," we read, "and wondered for joy."[4] It seemed to them, as our saying goes, "too good to be true." And, when He ate and drank with them, "none of them who were at meat durst ask Him, 'Who art Thou?' knowing that it was the Lord."[5]

[1] Matt. xxxvii. 63. [2] Luke xxiv. 11-23. [3] Luke xxiv. 37.
[4] Ibid. vers. 41. [5] John xxi. 12.

On His part, He rebukes them for their unbelief; shows them the print of the Wounds, in His Hands, and Feet, and Side; bids them to "handle and see" for themselves, that He is no spirit, but flesh and blood:[1] and then, as if to set at rest every suspicion of a mere vision, "He was seen by more than five hundred brethren at once."[2] And so they come gradually to put aside their dread, and are more at their ease in His sacred Presence; and, behaving quite like their former selves, they ask Him questions —as about John, if it were true that he was not to die, like the rest, but to abide on earth until His second Coming;[3] or if He would not "at this time restore the Kingdom to Israel."[4] Now, then, they do not merely *believe*, they *know*—that He is arisen.

Before I leave this portion of my subject, one word more upon it. I have compared, with the Resurrection of our Blessed Saviour, the resurrection of Lazarus; in its effect, that is to say, upon the mind and imagination of the eye-witnesses; but the comparison holds no further. Lazarus arose the same as before his death: it was open to the unbeliever, if he chose, to deny that the man had ever died. But Jesus arose changed. He appears again on earth, and in the flesh; but, it is as the inhabitant of another world. He enters into a room of which the doors are locked; He appears, and again suddenly vanishes out of sight. But that they "touch and handle," they might still suspect a spirit. He is

---

[1] Luke xxiv. 39.   [2] 1 Cor. xv. 6.
[3] John xxi. 21-23. [4] Acts i. 6.

living Man then,—that He puts beyond the shadow of a doubt; but One Who lives not in this world as in His home: His true home is in the unseen world, with the blessed Angels. He is the Witness of that Home which Lazarus was not. He is not as yet indeed ascended into Heaven, but He is due there. He must first be manifested as the Second Adam, in whom the dead live again, and as a proof that henceforth the grave cannot hold a son of man for ever; and when, after the forty days of His sojourn were expired, He ascends unto His place at the Father's Right Hand, it is as "the First Fruits of them that sleep."

No wonder, then, these things being so, that the head and front of the Apostle's preaching was: "Jesus hath God raised again from the dead, whereof all we are witnesses;"[1] together with that co-ordinate truth, that, as He is risen again, even so we, "if we have been planted together in the likeness of His death, we shall be also in the likeness of His Resurrection."[2] But example is more persuasive than preaching; and these first preachers shed their blood in witness of their words. Gladly they shed it; for, in the light of that Resurrection which they preached, death had lost its terrors. Henceforward, they look towards that consummation, not merely with hope, but with earnest longing. They desire "to be dissolved and to be with Christ," as "a thing, by far the better" than "to abide still in the flesh."[3] And, in the measure of their joy at the prospect of

---

[1] Acts ii. 32.   [2] Rom. vi. 4.   [3] Phil. i. 23.

death, is their contempt for the perishable goods of earth, as all "unworthy to be compared with the glory to come that shall be revealed in us:"[1] they "counted all things but as dung" that they might "gain Christ."[2]

Such was their teaching: Now as to its immediate effect on the world. With what joy to the poor, unenlightened heathen, came the glad tidings of Life and Light, through death and the grave! And the very men who announced to them this good news, that Jesus Christ, whom the Jews had slain, was alive, and that they should live in Him,—they had themselves seen and spoken, had eaten and drunk with Him, after He was arisen, or else had received the account from those who had witnessed these things, and had shed their blood for the word they had spoken. Henceforth (strange words!) welcome death and the grave! Welcome the rack, the cross, fire, or the sword, if only these could open a way to Christ and the immortal Home, which He had gone before to make ready for them. But, for vast numbers of them, it was not enough to wait until they were denounced, and die with patient courage, when their time was come; but, such was their zeal to die, that they provoked their own apprehension. They tore down edicts, or broke idols; they leaped into the arena of their own accord, exclaiming that they were Christians; they went before the magistrates, singly, or in a body, demanding to be proceeded against. Racks, pincers, rakes, hooks and gridirons

[1] Rom. viii. 18. [2] Phil. iii. 8.

—to be broken on the wheel, stretched with ropes and pulleys, plunged in boiling pitch, torn limb from limb by wild cattle—every, the most unheard-of form and shape of death, seemed only to add a relish to the passage. But enough; for these things are well known. In those days, it was almost the practical definition of a Christian, that he was one who courted death, and laughed tortures to scorn, when these things met him in the way of, what the world was pleased to call, his superstition.

And now, brethren, to pass from those ancient times to our own days, and to ourselves: why should not this blessed Truth be to us what it was to these first Christians? Or what manner of Christians are we, if death, though it come in never so mild and peaceful a shape, be a horror, which to them, though it came with violence and torture, was a boon and a joy? With us, as with them, it is the only way to the living and life-giving Christ. Were this not so, it were indeed a fearful thing to die. For what spectacle has earth more pitiful or ghastly than the death-chamber, if viewed with carnal eyes? What so sorry and unseemly sight, as that dull, cold clay, which seems what it is not! Such, for two short days or more, was once, as we have seen, the outward Christ, when suddenly He burst the tomb, and rose up again, in that very flesh that men had nailed to the Cross—a living Witness of a Life beyond the grave, the First Fruits of the ingathering of the harvest of Resurrection!

O then, my brethren, O Christian men and women,

if this be the gospel which we have received, and if indeed we have not believed in vain, how comes it we should ever think or behave as if our lofty faith were but an idle dream? How is it that, as a matter which may one day concern ourselves, we avoid the very name of death, or only allude thereto in slanting phrase as a "something which may happen;" or, if we speak outright, it is with coward lips and altered tone, as something so uttered it were best unuttered? How comes it that, when our beloved one is taken away to God's Rest, we still cleave to the idle dust with fruitless tears, or loiter at the tomb "seeking the living among the dead," superfluous in our grief, "sorrowing like them that have no hope?" How is it that, giving our high hope the lie, we are ourselves so tough-rooted here below that, with our every heart's fibre and with a grasp that still tightens with age, we cling to earth, and sadly watch the narrowing span of years, over-anxious about the body's health, ingeniously studious not to die? What ails us Christians of these latter days that our faith, attested by "such a cloud of witnesses," has become as a song without music, or a perfume that has lost its savour; that no longer, like them of old, we grieve that our sojourning is prolonged, but linger, loth to quit our ruining house of clay, while Christ has prepared for us incorruptible dwelling places in His heavenly Kingdom? "Alas," you answer, "we are not yet prepared to die;" and it is true: but is not this mainly because we dote on life and love this present world? Is not our overweening fondness for life and savour of earthly things at the root of all our unpreparedness? O then, let us be Christians in word and truth, and practise daily still to die to the world in spirit and affection. Since we have not an immortality here below, what other course is worthy reasonable men? Nor will it create in us a gloomy temper so to do; for how should it sadden the joys of life, while we cherish such of them as are pure and innocent, to be willing still to quit them for a brighter world above? Never let us seek the couch at night, save so disposed, that, if it be His Will who holds life's thread, we also be willing to wake no more—except to Him. So, when it is His Will, our round of days complete, shall we pass, like strong gladiators practised to the death. So shall death, which must come at last to all, find us willing and happy in our spirit. Quickly it will come; it will not tarry, for in its coming it will make equal the longest lifetime and the shortest. "Behold, I come quickly, and My reward is with Me, to render to every man according to his work. . . . Amen, come, Lord Jesus."[1]

[1] Apoc. xii. 20.

X.

THE RESURRECTION OF THE BODY.

"And as concerning the dead, that they rise again, have you not read in the book of Moses how in the bush God spake to him, saying, 'I am the God of Abraham, and the God of Isaac, and the God of Jacob.' He is not the God of the dead, but of the living. Ye do therefore greatly err."—MARK xii. 26, 27.

IT might be asked about this very remarkable argument of our Blessed Saviour, how it was really a proof of the Resurrection of the Body? We might imagine the Sadducees (for to them the argument was addressed) objecting that, because God is called in Scripture the God of Abraham, Isaac, and Jacob, it followed indeed that these holy patriarchs existed somewhere, although their bodies were dead. Their bodies lay in the tomb, but their spirits were still alive, and God was still the God of these blessed spirits, and they were still His servants; but how did this go to show that their *bodies* would rise again from the dead? The question is so very obvious that I think there must be some good reason why the cavillers did not put it, but felt themselves answered by our Lord's argument. God is the God of Abraham, Isaac, and Jacob: therefore Abraham, Isaac, and Jacob still lived; and their bodies would rise again at the Last Day, since He is not the God of the dead, but of the living. And St. Luke adds to the account of the discussion, that "some of the Scribes answering said to Him: 'Master, Thou hast well said.' And, after that, they durst not ask Him any more questions."[1]

The reason, I think, is this, that the Jew never separated in his thought the immortality of the soul from the Resurrection of the Body. The heathen would prove the immortality of the soul by his philosophy; but he had no notion of the Resurrection of the Body; or, if he had any such notion, he did not conclude it by his philosophy, but it came to him by the way of tradition. Whereas, with the Jew it was otherwise. He did not acquire religion by philosophy, but he received it from divine Revelation. This revelation spoke to him of a Redeemer to come, who would do away the mischief of Adam's sin, which brought death into the world. Now, it is the work of death to sunder the body from the soul; and, therefore, it was to be the work of the Redeemer to conquer death by restoring the soul to the body. And hence it is that holy Job, who, though not a Jew, had received, through tradition, the revelation of God, exclaims, "I know that my Redeemer liveth, and in the Last Day I shall rise out of the earth . . . and *in my flesh* I shall see God."[2]

[1] Luke xx. 39, 40.   [2] Job xix. 25, 26.

This, then, most likely, was the reason that the Sadducees had no rejoinder to our Lord's answer that God was the God, not of the dead, but of the living. If Abraham, and Isaac, and Jacob lived *at all*, they would rise again in their bodies: there was no doubt about that, to the mind of a Jew. As to the doctrine of the immortality of the soul, *apart* from the Resurrection of the Body, it was a sheer heathen notion, which would hardly have been entertained for a moment by one who had received the comforting teaching of a Resurrection. For such a one, the denial of the Resurrection would be equivalent to the denial of any state of existence whatsoever after death; and hence St Paul argues, that if there be no Resurrection in Christ, that "then they also who are fallen asleep in Christ *are perished*."[1]

Now, the fact that our Blessed Saviour's argument considers the doctrines of the immortality of the soul and the Resurrection of the Body as portions of one dogma, so as to take it for granted that no man (who had heard of both) would think of holding the one, while denying the other, is a fact well deserving of notice, and one, I think, which may be profitably enlarged upon.

Body and soul, and the interests of body and soul, are more nearly related than perhaps is generally considered. Thus, man is not a merely intellectual creature, like the angels, nor a merely animal creature, like the brutes; but he consists of body and soul, united in one person. This personality, it is

---

[1] 1 Cor. xv. 18.

true, has its root and origin in the soul, rather than in the body. For it is the soul which makes a man to be alive, and to be one and individual. It is the soul which binds into sympathy and harmony the several parts and members of the body, and all together with itself, so as to make a man to be, and to feel himself, strictly one and identical. But it is also equally true that the body, by being brought into union with the soul, is made to share in its personality; so that a man becomes, body and soul, one person in *two* natures.

And while so strict is the union of body and soul in man, equally strict is also their corresponding mutual dependence and intercourse. If the soul is a power, the body is its instrument; if the soul is intelligent, it is the bodily senses which furnish it with the very objects on which its intelligence is exercised; if it is the nature of the soul to desire love, and admire, it is through the eye, ear, taste, or touch of the body that it seeks and finds what it wishes, loves, or admires. And if the soul is beautiful, it is the body which is the manifestation of its beauty. We cannot see the soul of our friend; it is the figure, the gesture, the plastic features, the eloquent glance, the playful lip, the tone of voice, which reveal him. We identify him with these; and the body which we see stands as the representative of the soul which we do not see. Indeed, we have, at first, to be taught that the body is not simply himself, and that he has a soul.

Now, who that considers this present connection

and intimacy of soul and body, their sympathy and mutual dependence, their conjoint fortunes in life, and considers likewise that it was the original purpose of God, in the creation of man, that body and soul should never be sundered for everlasting—that man should be immortal; and further that, whereas sin interfered with this divine purpose, bringing the corruption of death into the world, yet the promised Redeemer was to vanquish sin, and deliver man from the power of death—who, I say, that duly considers these things, would hesitate to regard the immortality of the soul and the Resurrection of the Body as inseparable truths? The heathen might indulge the natural fancy of a dim, shadowy after-world, wherein pensive ghosts of men, with thin, small voices, and transparent frames, wandered with noiseless footfall in unsubstantial realms of light and gloom, pondering their lives past, and deeds wrought in the flesh; met and parted, exchanged converse in terms of love or hate—imitating the drama of life. But not so the Jew, if at least he realised the divine economy as declared in Holy Scripture, and realised the power of God, which was able to quicken even the dust and ashes of our mortal bodies. Hence it was that our Lord rebuked the questioners, asking them, "Do ye not therefore err because ye know not the Scriptures nor the power of God? . . . He is not the God of the dead, but of the living; for all live unto Him: ye do therefore greatly err."[1]

[1] Mark xii 24; Luke xx. 38.

In the eyes of men the holy Patriarchs were dead, because their souls were separated from their bodies, which separation constitutes the notion of death; but in the eye of God's purpose, they still lived, as all live to Him. He "calleth the things that are not as those that are," because of His purpose, and the power of His Word to make them be. He sees that the souls of the dead, though they be now separated from, are due to, their bodies; and hence their bodies are not as dead, to Him, but rather as sleepers whom He will, sometime, arouse. And He sees the end and issue of a law which has already gone forth to bid them live again—a law which is already in operation.

For, brethren, the reunion of the souls with the bodies of the dead is even now in course of preparation: the very corruption of death itself is already preparing it. Nothing defiled can enter Heaven. But while the penal fires are purging the soul of the just man departed, to fit him for the blessed vision of God, is there no purgatorial cleansing likewise for the body, the unfortunate accomplice of its sin? defiled and unholy, scarred, loathsome, deformed and degraded in it? Yes, there is such cleansing, for the body as for the soul; and this cleansing is wrought in it by the corruption of death itself. And as in bodily sickness, it happens oftentimes that health is recovered by means of the very symptoms of the disease; so it is in this case. The law of corruption works itself out, and exhausts itself, in such a manner, that at last nothing is left to corrupt. The body is no longer body; the various members, tissues, membranes, muscles, sinews, bones, being resolved into their component dust. Nay, the very dust itself ceases, being resolved into those primal atoms and mere seeds of being called substances, which no man can see, or touch, or smell, or discern at all by the senses; nor can any man describe them, or say what they are, but only that they must exist, as the constitutive forces and causes of that matter which is discerned by the senses.

Such is the Purgatory of the body in death, and so thoroughly done its work, that no trace of sinful contact from its former fellowship with the soul remains to it. And if the sacred Body of our Blessed Saviour was not suffered to see corruption, and if tradition affirms the same of the immaculate body of His Blessed Mother; and if, likewise, the bodies of many saints have been preserved to us in various degrees of incorruption, perhaps it is a law that where there has been no sinful stain upon the soul, there should be no corresponding corruption of the body; and that there should be degrees of corruption.

Thus, while the souls of the just departed are in the hand of God, their bodies are gathered, through the law of death, into the common womb of nature. And should any captious, curious mind amuse itself with the conceit that, perchance still subject to the laws of nature, their atom seeds may germinate again as man once more, or bird or beast, or fish or flowering herb, this seems to be but an idle fancy; for what do we really know as regards God's hidden world of *substances?* Or, do not such persons greatly err as understanding not the Scriptures, nor the power of God? Say rather that the atom relics of the just, withdrawn from the rule of nature, are obedient to the Word of God, and consigned to the ministry of angels. For the wardship of the dead and ministry in the Resurrection are attributed in holy Scripture to these blessed spirits.[1] And at the Last Day they shall surrender their charge: and then " in a moment, in the twinkling of an eye, at the last trumpet: for the trumpet shall sound, and the dead shall rise again incorruptible, and we shall be changed. For this corruptible must put on incorruption, and this mortal must put on immortality."[2] Then shall the soul, which has been proved in the Fire of Judgment, be restored to the body, which has been cleansed in the sifting process of dissolution.

But the garment of the flesh will not be merely restored, in the case of the just it will be renewed by the power of God, so as to be the suitable habitation of the renewed spirit. And who shall tell the glory of this renewal? If the mortal body be so admirable a vessel and instrument of the soul in its godlike front and stature erect; in the symmetry of its shapely members; in the ever-varying grace and rhythm of its movements; in the subtle language of

---

[1] Matt. xxiv. 31; Jude ix.   [2] 1 Cor xv. 52, 53.

the eye and features; and the unmatched music of speech—what, then, shall it become in the day of its incorruptible immortality? The Almighty Creator has sometimes endowed the human body, even in its present lowly condition, with such gifts of beauty and gracefulness as none can consider unmoved. And if this be a painful subject (and it is a painful subject, when we reflect how the gift has been perverted to serve the purposes of vanity and sin), this fact speaks nothing against the gift itself, or its significance. It is true that we are told to hate our body here on earth, but that is only that we may save it for hereafter. "He that loveth his life shall lose it; and he that hateth his life in this world keepeth it unto life eternal." Holy Scripture insists, on the other hand, upon the dignity and honour of the body as the vessel of an immortal soul, and the living temple of the Holy Ghost. So, when the soul is restored to honour, shall the body also, in God's good time, be restored to honour with it. Then instead of being burdensome, it shall be free as the soul itself; instead of a hindrance it shall be a help; instead of weakness it shall be girt on with strength; instead of shame and confusion it shall be clothed with light and glory.

Thoughts like these, my brethren, ought to raise our hope to the highest measure of human consolation; they should be a powerful assistance to us in the conquering of that natural dread of death which must, however shortly (God knows how shortly), be with us, whether or not we shall have been enabled to reconcile ourselves to it. For who would not bear the momentary throes and stifling distress and anguish of dissolution, commit his body to the dust, and his soul even to the flaming sword which guards the return to Paradise, supported by so glorious a prospect as this: To know and converse with the gracious, loving Person of Jesus Christ; to be admitted amongst the circle of His chosen ones; to see the blessed faces of those saints whose records have already taught us to know and love them; and what, though last, is not a little, to meet again those friends departed whose love and sympathy was a wealth of the heart incomparably greater than all the treasures of earth, and to recognise them by the same familiar tokens as upon earth, saving that every defect shall be compensated, every deformity straightened, every blemish removed, and every tear wiped away for ever? Death is indeed a solemn, serious thought; but when we consider these things, it ought not surely to be a gloomy or painful one. The more we think about it the more it will bear thinking about. The worldling may well shrink and quake when that which he feared shall have come to pass, and when he is forced to face that, as a reality, the thought of which he had always studiously put away from him; when the light of the eyes is darkened and the idols of his worship are broken; but not so we, if indeed "we have turned" from the idols of this world "to serve the living and true God, and to wait for His Son from Heaven Whom He raised up from the dead," as a type and earnest of our own raising, "Jesus Who hath delivered us from the wrath to come."[1]

[1] Thess. i. 9, 10.

XI.

THE PENITENTIAL SPIRIT.

"For you were as sheep going astray; but you are now converted to the Shepherd and Bishop of your souls."—1 PET. ii. 25.

MAY I not address you, brethren, in the language of St. Peter (at least the words are applicable to many amongst you), and say that, Whereas you had been like sheep going astray, you are now converted to the Shepherd and Bishop of your souls? For why does the Church address you (since it is not merely I, but the Church which addresses you) as converts, but because she judges that you are such in very truth. It is scarcely two weeks ago since she set before you the Image of your crucified Saviour, that the sight of that wounded heart might subdue the obduracy of your own. It is but a short time ago also that she led you out of the busy world into the wilderness of a spiritual Retreat, where there was silence of every voice save the Voice of God. Because, for a time, man spoke not, or he only spoke of God; and so it was rather God Who spoke than man. And then, in that quiet and solitude of silence, God came near to you—so near that you knew, you felt it was none but He, and He set you before His Face, and you trembled at His awful Holiness. It seemed as if you had never before really known what God was, nor felt what it *meant* that there was a God; that we were His creatures; and that, put Him out of sight as we may, He is, after all, the great Reality, and we must have Him or perish.

Then did He set your own self before yourself; and you saw, as in a glass, your own face, how uncomely and unsightly sin had made it. He unrolled, before the eyes of your soul, the vision of your life, in many scenes, ordered in succession of times, from childhood upwards, with different persons engaged therein, but always one chief actor—Yourself. He "set your iniquities before His Eyes, and your life in the light of His Countenance." He showed you how so early, when you had begun to know Him, you had strayed away from His side; you had left His Way, and chosen for yourself crooked, thorny ways of your own; you had turned your back on the peace and abundance of His house to feed on husks of swine and the garbage of sin. He counted out your sins before you, each one, with its special tokens of malice or aggravation; and, as He counted, a witness rose up against you from within, and confirmed the words of God—your Conscience, as it were another Self, and reproached you with unutterable bitterness.

But then, while you shrunk within yourself in

terror and dismay; while you were bowed to earth in confusion and abasement; while your heart within you was wrung with excess of sorrow and anguish, He did not repel; He did not reproach; He did not despise; He spoke not of wrath, but of mercy; He spoke not of retribution, but of forgiveness. Like the Prodigal returning home, you had approached Him on bended knee; but He uplifted and caught you in His arms; and as you buried your face in His bosom, He soothed you with words of love and tenderness. And fain you would have said, "Father, I have sinned against heaven and before Thee: I am not now worthy to be called Thy son; make me as one of Thy hired servants;" but the words died away on your lips as you felt, by the warmth of His embrace, that He was ever the same loving Father, and only your miserable self had suffered change.

Then there fell upon you that calm of which worldlings never dreamed, the peace of God "which passeth understanding;" and those tears flowed from the eyes, so sweet in the shedding, out of the fulness of heart which knows no void, and pleasure which leaves no sting. There was joy in Heaven as upon earth; for the angels were hymning their hymns of praise and thanksgiving before the Lord, Who had commanded them, saying: Rejoice with Me, "because this My son was dead, and he is come to life again; he was lost, and he is found." Oh, happy day of conversion! It seemed as though the music of the angels was heard even upon earth, and the earth gladdened beneath the smile of God. The very sunlight was brighter and holier. The returning colours of the landscape, the merry voices of the birds, the very breath of the spring-tide air was fraught with the Benediction of God.

But why do I dwell on the past? Why do I read to you, my brethren, your feelings of a week or so ago, when I should rather be engaged with laying down some rule for present trial, or some counsel for the future, which might be profitable for us all? This is the reason then: I would that we should learn, from what is past, a lesson available for the present and the future: and therefore, I take it, the Church reminds us to-day of our old selves, and that we were as sheep going astray; but now we are returned to the Shepherd and Bishop of our souls.

For the past has its lesson for us, and would that we could always remember it, would that (if I may so express myself) we could always remain converts, in retaining the Spirit of Penitence; as King David remained always a convert, and, although he was pardoned, and he knew that he was pardoned, yet was it ever his delight to evoke, from the ashes of the past, the ghost of his old self! He was already cleansed, and he knew it; but he ever cried out: "Wash me yet more from mine iniquity, and cleanse me from my sin." . . . "Thou shalt sprinkle me with hyssop, and I shall be cleansed; Thou shalt wash me, and I shall be made whiter than snow;"[1] and

[1] Ps. l. 4, 9.

"I have laboured in my groanings: every night I will wash my bed, I will water my couch with my tears."[1] And indeed, what safer precaution, to avoid falling again, than the consideration that he had fallen before, and that when he most imagined himself secure? How he would tremble at the thought of his own frailty, and cleave with vehemence to the hand of his Almighty Father, crying: "Cast me not away from Thy Face, and take not Thy Holy Spirit from me." ... "Turn not away Thy Face from me: in the day when I am in trouble, incline Thine ear to me." ... "In what day soever I shall call upon Thee, hear me speedily."[2]

Would that we could always remain converts, like Magdalen, who loved her place at the Feet of our Lord, and would not change it, but there clung for refuge, there wept and embraced; and who, as the legend tells, when He was gone to His glory, never rejoiced, as one who had a right to rejoice, or rejoiced only in tears, and wept her sweet life away in seclusion; or like St. Peter—Oh, what a lesson! He was to be the Rock and bulwark of the Church's strength, yet God would not trust Him, until he had learnt the great lesson of how little he was to be trusted. And he also, tradition says, bore ever in his mind the memory of his weakness, and, even until old age, still wept at the crowing of the cock, and was kept standing by his fear of falling; or like St. Paul, who exclaims, "Who is weak and I am not weak?" who called himself the "least of the apostles," and "not

[1] Ps. vi. 7. [2] Ibid. l. 12; ci. 2, 3.

worthy to be called an apostle," because he had persecuted the Church of God; and who, as he tells us, "chastised his body, and brought it into subjection, lest perhaps when he had preached to others, he might himself become a castaway."[1] Indeed, so it seems with all the convert saints (for I do not wish to advance anything for mere theory's sake); such was the case with St. Thaïs, St. Mary of Egypt, St. Augustine, our own St. Thomas of Canterbury, and all the great converts—converts they were, and converts they remained through life: our very idea of them is associated with their conversion.

And what wonder if they thus retained for ever the spirit and attitude of penitence, knowing God as He had made them to know Him, and regarding their sins in the white light of His Holiness. "Since God is so good and holy," they would say, "and yet so tender, merciful and compassionate—what then am I, who sinned against Him, as I have sinned? I am not fit to live, or look up into the sweet heavens. Henceforth I am hateful in my own sight; nor let any man think me white and clean, while I am what I am before God: I denounce myself before the whole world, and only desire to be dealt with according to my deserts. I have now but one end and aim in life, to weep away my life, in the lowest place, and punish myself for my sin." If this be the language (and it *is*, in substance, the language) of convert saints, it appears that the Spirit of Penitence is, in the very nature of the case, *abiding*.

[1] 1 Cor. ix. 27.

Let us now see how we can turn these considerations into some practical benefit for ourselves.

And first, as there is a sense in which we should always, so to speak, remain converts, so also, in another sense, the rest of our life will differ widely, as a general rule, from its state at the period of our conversion. For the time of conversion, as a rule, is a time of consolation, while our life, on the whole, is a time of probation. Or better: our whole life is absolutely a period of probation; but God proves persons, as it has been said,[1] "in two ways—by *consolation* and by *tribulation*;" and both these ways are ordered to our advantage by a wise dispensation of providence—tribulation, lest we should presume, but consolation, lest we should despair. Trust me, then, brethren, your present feelings of devotion (but observe, I speak of mere feelings) will not continue. They were good, and perhaps necessary for you at the time; but they will have answered the end which your Heavenly Father had in view, and then they will die away. The day of trial will come: perhaps you feel that it has come already. Perhaps, in the fervour of conversion, you had said within yourself, ".How came I ever to have fallen into such or such a sin? I was blind; I was infatuated. At any rate *now*, at last, I see things clearly. Surely it is impossible that the like courses or company should ever delude me again. Henceforward I will be my better self; I will break with evil companions; I will throw all human respects to the winds, and act with

[1] Imitation III., cap. 3, 5.

independence. Instead of being led by others, I will lead and give the tone myself; at least I shall be respected: perchance I shall do much good." Nay, some one or other might go further still and say in his heart, "I fell into considerable sins formerly; for I am a man of strong, headlong passions, and I was hard pressed by temptation; but now, thank God, He has been pleased to work such a change in me that I am quite a different being, and the past is only like a bad dream: *Laqueus contritus est;* at last I am safe."

Oh, my brethren, you are blind indeed—you are indeed infatuated, if you reason thus with yourselves. May God preserve us from sin; but do not say there is no danger. Be not a convert after your own fashion, but be converted as Holy David, as Magdalen, as St. Peter, and St. Paul were converted. Evoke, from the grave in your bosom where you have buried him, the dead *self* of yesterday, and ask him how he came to fall away. "Oh," he will answer, "I trusted all was going well with me (and so it was, for aught I knew to the contrary), and so I was off my guard; and temptation took me by surprise, on a sudden, and I fell: and once down, it was no easy matter to rise again, but I was led on from one thing to another; and thus I became what I was." What, then, is a man never safe from falling? Oh yes; but never safer than when he fears to fall; for fearing to fall we shall cleave to God, and leaning on God we shall not fall; for "God is faithful, Who will not suffer you to be tempted above that which you are able;

K

but will make, also with temptation, issue, that you may be able to bear it." [1]

And then there are other trials, besides temptation, to which the same principle is applicable. How easy, in the season of conversion, seemed to us the service of God! how pleasant His worship! what visitations in time of prayer! what a charm in Holy Communion! Ah, it goes hard with us to put up with the truth in these matters! But, surely, brethren, you know that, unless yours is a very unusual case indeed, this state of things will only last for a while. And better it should not: God consults your own welfare when He disposes otherwise. He will prove you, if you love Him with all your heart. And the time will come when you will find it hard to pray, when you cannot collect your thoughts, when your feelings will become parched, and your spiritual faculties will be darkened. And perhaps just at that time the Tempter will come to you, and will urge that, after all, the promise of religion was fairer than the performance; that God cares not for you; that, anyhow, you are unhappy and perplexed, and that, whereas you have been striving, as best you could, to lead a holy life, you, at least, are not to blame. What then, will you begin to murmur and complain, as though God had dealt unfairly with you? And who are we, my brethren, that we should presume to dictate to the Almighty the conditions of the service which we owe to Him? and say to Him, in effect, if not in so many words: " I would fain serve Thee,

[1] 1 Cor. x. 13.

Lord, yet not in Thy way, but in mine own; for Thy way is very hard to me, and I am sorely tried. I am distracted with occupations; I am beset with perplexities; I am devoured with cares and troubles; I am dejected with ill-health; I am tempted; I am forlorn: Take the load from off my back, and I will serve Thee!" But are we not sinners? Have we not deserved hell? Is it nothing that God suffers us to approach Him, to sit down amongst His household, to count us amongst His friends, yea amongst His children; when, had not His mercy intervened, we had already been cast into the outer darkness? Are not the very troubles which we lament, and magnify so much, blessings in disguise, so many cords of necessity, by which He would bind us closer to Himself, through the very sense of our own insufficiency? Oh peevish, wayward, restless hearts! Let us know our place: let us embrace His sacred Feet! Let us lay our burden before Him, and tell Him that it is not so great, by a hundredfold, as we have deserved for our sins. He will give us strength to bear it, He will make His yoke sweet, and His burden light. Perhaps He will lighten us of half of it; but only as it accords with His own all-wise designs; and when He knows that it will be best for us; and not merely to answer our own narrow views, and our fretful impatience, which makes us sometimes ask Him we know not what.

Thus, brethren, let us imitate the convert saints in retaining the spirit of conversion. Let us meditate our unworthiness, and hate our past life all the more, as this will enable us to live more worthily for the future. And by how much more we are unable to help ourselves, let us call upon God for His help. Let us not be surprised at our ordinary failings; for we are sinners. Let us not be surprised if the consolations of the spiritual life are not always our portion; nor be hurt if others slight us, if we are not loved or admired, if our defects are cast in our teeth; for we are sinners. How can we expect others to esteem us, when we have ceased to esteem ourselves? This is the exalted humility of the saints. We shall hardly rival them in it; for it is very contrary to flesh and blood. Still God has raised them up to be our models, and we must strive to imitate them. So shall we have made a good and fruitful retreat.

XII.

THE BREAD OF LIFE.

"I am the Living Bread which came down from Heaven. If any man eat of this Bread, he shall live for ever; and the Bread which I will give is My Flesh for the life of the world."—JOHN vi. 51, 52.

I SUPPOSE that, in reading these words, it scarcely enters into our minds that the natural life of the body is spoken of at all. We take it for granted that our Blessed Saviour speaks, in this place, of the life of the soul only—of the supernatural life of divine grace. But when we come to weigh the matter well, and compare this with other passages of Holy Scripture, I think we shall find that the Bread of Life is such to the whole man, both soul and body; though, of course, it is chiefly, and in the first place, the food of the soul. In proof of this statement, observe:

That when our Lord speaks of Himself as the Bread of Life, He makes allusion to the death of the body, which is, next to sin, the greatest evil in the world: "Your fathers did eat manna in the desert, and are dead. This is the Bread which cometh down from Heaven, that, if any man eat of it, he may not die;" but this reference to the natural death would be irrelevant, were not the Bread, in some sort, a remedy for it. And in what manner it is a remedy is further declared in these words: "He that eateth My Flesh and drinketh My Blood hath everlasting Life, and I will raise him up in the Last Day."[1] And to the same purpose, the Eucharistic Bread is compared in Holy Scripture to the fruit of the Tree of Life, which was to have rendered our First Parents immortal, had they not eaten of the Tree of Knowledge instead. For, speaking of the heavenly Jerusalem, which is the Church of God, St. John says: "In the midst of the street thereof, and on both sides of the river, was the Tree of Life, bearing twelve fruits . . . and the leaves of the tree were for the healing of the nations."[2] The Holy Eucharist has therefore been understood by doctors of the Church to be, not only a pledge of future glory, but, as it were, the seed of immortality and glorious resurrection to the body into which it has been worthily received; though such effect, it is almost needless to say, is limited to the just who depart this life in God's favour, because to the unjust there is resurrection indeed, but not of glory.

But if it be asked, How fares it then with them that, through no fault of their own, die without ever having tasted of the heavenly Bread; shall there be for all such no glorious resurrection? I answer that

[1] John vi. 50, 55. [2] Apoc. xxii. 2.

doubtless Almighty God, out of the infinite wealth of His resources, has made provision for such, as indeed He has made provision for such as, through no fault of their own, are debarred from the use of other sacraments. The glorified Body of Christ may, for aught we know to the contrary, be really applied, after some hidden manner, to the departed just, who have never had the unspeakable advantage of receiving it sacramentally. But however this may be, since God has appointed that we ourselves be quickened by the reception of the Holy Eucharist, it cannot concern us, save as a matter of speculation, how all others are quickened that wait upon their Lord and walk in His steps. I shall therefore give no further answer to this question. But there is another question which you may ask, brethren, which I will answer, because it does concern ourselves, and also because the answer may prove instructive and of practical benefit. It is this:

If the Holy Eucharist is in truth the Bread of Life and seed of immortality, how comes it that we eat thereof, and yet, in the natural course, we die? It does not arrest the decay of the body; it does not heal its disorders, and though it strengthens in the last agony, it does not bid that chalice pass by, but each of us must drink it, even to the dregs. How then, it may be asked, is the Holy Eucharist the remedy for death? I answer that it is the remedy for death in the same sense in which the sin of our First Parents was the cause of death. Moreover, the order and manner of the remedy answer exactly to the order and manner of the evil which was to be cured. See then, what was the order and manner of the evil. The Tree of Knowledge was the tree of death. God had charged Adam that, "In what day soever thou shalt eat of it, thou shalt die the death."[1] They ate of the fruit, Adam and Eve; but they did not die the death of the body in the day of their eating: they died in the natural course. How then did they die as God had threatened? They died the death of the soul. They did not lose at once the natural life whereby man lives; but they did lose at once the supernatural life whereby he lives to God. This was, in the first place, the death wherewith they were threatened; the other, the death of the body, would follow in due course, and as a consequence. And just as it was then said of the forbidden fruit, "In what day soever thou shalt eat of it, thou shalt die the death," so is it now said of the Bread of Life, that, "If any man eat of this Bread, he shall live for ever." Thus the divine Life was lost in the First Adam, and corruption followed, which wrought to the death of the body; and now the same divine Life is restored in the Second Adam, which works, through the Holy Sacrament as the source of incorruption, unto immortality. And thus the manner of the remedy corresponds to the manner of the malady which was to be cured.

Are then, it will be asked, the words "life" and "death," as applied to the present subject, to be used in a different meaning from that in which we com-

[1] Gen. ii. 17.

monly use them? Well, in one sense, they are: for Life, in Holy Scripture, is emphatically the divine Life, and death the loss of the divine Life. But is not the very fact that the words are so used intended to show us that there is a closer connection between sin and death and between life and grace than men commonly think? For what was death to Adam? Was it merely the separation of the body from the living principle which quickens it? No: Adam did not merely die the death of nature, because he did not merely live the life of nature: he received from God Himself the divine Life of grace. This is signified by the fact that "The Lord God," as we read, "breathed into the face" of Adam "the breath of life, and man became a living soul."[1] Now it was to this divine Life, when nourished by the Tree of Life, that was attached the gift of immortality. Had man merely lived the life of the beasts, he had perished with them; but by virtue of the divine Life which he received from God, he was to have been immortal —had he not sinned. This is the account of death in Holy Scripture. It is not merely, as men speak, "the debt of nature;" for God made not man subject to the law of nature. "God made man incorruptible," it is written, "and to the image of His own Likeness He made him; but by the envy of the devil, death came into the world."[2] It is a debt incurred by the loss of divine grace. Such is the notion of life, and such the notion of death implied by the Word of God,—that life, everlasting Life, is

[1] Gen. ii. 7. [2] Wisd. ii. 23, 24.

the divine Life of grace, and that death, originally, is the consequence of sin.

And not only originally, but also actually, it may be said, is death the consequence of sin. For although, since the divorce in Adam of the divine from the natural life, men would necessarily die, in the course of nature; yet, as a matter of fact, how few, if really any, die in the course of nature. Scarcely will you find a constitution so robust, so finely organised and tempered, so well-balanced and equable, but it bears within it the seeds of disease which are gradually ripening unto death. And disease, is it not of sin? At any rate, we cannot shut our eyes to the fact of the fearful havoc which sin is making in the bodies, as well as in the souls of men. Were there in the world a race or family unacquainted with sin, either in itself or in its effects, such a race or family would surely differ widely from any that we see in the world around us. But observe that I do not mean that every kind of sin directly conduces to the destruction of the body, as, for instance, intemperance conduces to it: it would be absurd to say so. I only wish to state the broad and general truth which stares us in the face; that unruly passions beget irregular habits, and irregular habits disorder nature; that a disordered nature poisons the life-blood of humanity, through inheritance; and hence a race of men with morbid, craving, sinful appetites, further fostered by indulgence. And hence it is that the whole tree of humanity, sin-poisoned as it is, bears so heavy a harvest of death. How many thousands of human beings perish in the very bud! How many thousands of young men and maidens suddenly fall off from their first promise, and belying the hope of their strength and beauty, wither in their blossom, blighted by hereditary taint! How many thousands more survive only to wear out a crippled, stunted life, or a life which is only one long struggle with death, till death at length prevails! How small and inconsiderable indeed is the number of those whom one might single out as fitting specimens and exemplars, in mind and body, of human nature!

The world being thus, as it were, in ruins, what is the remedy? Our First Parents ate of the tree of death: behold, brethren, the Tree of Life is within your reach, eat and ye shall live! I say not indeed that you shall live the present, poisoned life of sorrow and shame; what soul which rightly understands its heaven-born origin would desire such a remedy? No: the remedy is one which begins at the beginning, which strikes at once at the root of the mischief, by nourishing that divine Life in the soul, the forfeiture of which was the origin of death to the body; and the glorious resurrection in the great Day will be its last and crowning result. And even now, do you not see, brethren, that its actual working is hostile to death? For it stimulates with divine fervours the spiritual powers of the soul, and strengthens the high hand of the will against those passions which minister to death; nay, even the body is refreshed oftentimes, and strengthened by the devout reception of these sacred mysteries. Such effects plainly indicate what is the tendency of the Sacrament. And if it do not bestow on us immortality at once, this is only because grace, like nature, has its laws. Man, having fallen from a higher to a lower scale, in the order of creation, which is subject to the law of death, to death he is due. The Son of God, it is true, has ransomed him to everlasting Life; but there is no entrance into the new save by egress out of the old life. So it is throughout the natural world. Life will not renew a withered or crippled limb, however warm and vigorous be the current of the blood. The leaves of a tree which have suffered blight never recover so as to resemble perfect leaves; but the sap which flows through their veins only serves to nourish a stunted, shapeless growth. And so with the divine Life: grace cannot restore the integrity of manhood, as it was lost in Adam, save only through death; but so long as we live, we must bear in soul and body the seams and scars of sin. Yet have faith, brethren. If indeed your souls and bodies are nourished by the Heavenly Bread, already Life everlasting has begun in you, and is working according to the measure of each one's co-operation, towards its fulfilment. For it was not said, observe, of him that eateth, that he *shall have* everlasting Life, but that he *hath* it. We have it: what, then, hinders its manifestation, but "the body of this death?" We are, in this respect, like those worms which feed on the sedges by the river's margin; but which are other than they appear. For their present life is but the bud and promise of their perfect being.

So, even while they seem to stiffen in the rigidity of death, the inner, higher life fermenting, bursts the outward husk of what they are; and unsightly grubs are transformed into a joyous, airy race that, with wings of gauze and rainbow hues, sparkle amongst the reeds and flash upon the waters. Such is a parable of our condition. We, too, are other than we seem; but that which is in us of corruption must perish before that which is of incorruption be revealed. We must die, that we may truly live, or rather that the Life everlasting within us may be made manifest. Is this strange, that death should be the means of life? that God should quicken the dust? What know we of life or death, of how God creates, or how He new-creates? Enough that there is given us the inestimable privilege of sitting down to the banquet of Life in the Holy Sacrament, and of knowing that, in receiving Jesus Christ into our mortal bodies, we are clothing them with His immortality; we are putting on His glory. And as His own glory was only made manifest through death, so with all of us who are glorified in Him: we must first die; but one day the glory which He has given us shall be manifested to the whole world. It *is now*, and it *shall be*, manifested.

And, my brethren, do we ponder, as we ought, these saving truths? Do we really understand what great and holy things surround us in the Church of God? What wealth unspeakable is ours, if only we will appropriate it? But observe that this is a treasure which is spiritually discerned, while the false goods of this world are tricked out to catch the eye; it is, however, none the less real on that account. So it was in the beginning. Not of the Tree of Life was it written, that its fruit was "fair to the eyes, and delightful to behold." No enlargement of knowledge or intoxication of the senses was promised to the eating thereof. Yet it was the Tree of Life, and that other one, whatsoever it promised, was the Tree of Death. And as it was then so is it now, that men overlook the Tree of Life, while they eat the bread and drink the wine of sin to the ruin of soul and body. But we, brethren, who have been taught better things—fools, if we are so much in love with this life-in-death as to set it before immortality; if we prefer "the husks that swine do eat" to the banquet of gods! Let us rather evermore hunger and thirst after this heavenly Food; let us evermore pray and strive that no impediment on our part may frustrate in us its life-giving operation; and while we raise up our hearts in thanksgiving to the God of mercies for this greatest of all His gifts in the institution of this Holy Sacrament, let us also enlarge the bowels of our charity on behalf of those who disbelieve, and beg that God would change their heart of unbelief, and bring them to that last of blessings recorded in the written Word: "Blessed are they that wash their robes in the Blood of the Lamb, that they may have a right to the Tree of Life, and may enter in by the gates of the City. . . . And the Spirit and the Bride say, Come. And he that heareth let him say, Come. And he that thirsteth let him come; and he that will, let him take the water of life, freely."[1]

[1] Apoc. xxii. 14, 17.

XIII.

TIME AND ETERNITY.

"But of this one thing be not ignorant, beloved, that one day, with the Lord, is as a thousand years, and a thousand years as one day."—2 PET. iii. 8.

THE term of our Blessed Saviour's absence designated in to-day's Gospel as "a little while," if we regard the primary sense of the words, is, no doubt, the brief interval between His death and glorious resurrection; but the consideration of the whole context in which the words occur, the customary usage of Holy Scripture, which speaks of the longest time as short, and the very fact that this gospel is selected for our instruction, in these latter days, point to a broader signification of our Lord's words, which adapts them to our day of expectation, of which the Apostle speaks in the self-same phrase: "A little while and a very little while, and He that is to come shall come, and will not delay;"[1] when the present "distress" and the world's

[1] Heb. x. 37.

vain triumph shall alike be ended, and our sorrows be exchanged for joy that will never cease. From this point of view, therefore, I will speak to you, brethren, this morning of the "little while" of Time, which is our mortal measure of duration, as compared with that other and divine measure which we name Eternity.

What men chiefly complain of in the goods of this world, is not merely their insufficiency (though they are insufficient), but that they do not endure. All of us have had our happy days, or months, or even years: we sigh when we think of them; but they are past and gone. There are, for most of us, we trust, many happy days in store, but even while we enjoy them, we shall sigh again to think that they will pass like the former. The interest of to-day will not interest a year hence; the friends of to-day will go, at length, to join the happy band of those who smile upon us from the ghostly Past. We are hurried along through the scenes of life with a speed we cannot realise: it is like the rapidity of modern travel, in which we are only made aware of our own movement by the suddenness with which objects are hurried out of sight. Men have devised certain considerations wherewith to console themselves for the shortness of Time: Time flies, says the worldling: let it go. "Let us enjoy the good things that are present . . . let us fill ourselves with costly wines and ointments; and let not the flower of the time pass by us. Let us crown ourselves with roses, ere they be withered: let no meadow escape our riot."[1] But

[1] Wisd. ii. 6-8.

the flowers of yesterday's banquet are a sorry sight, and the echo of yesterday's laughter has a mournful ring. The wisdom of the world is all foolishness before God; but the philosophy of worldlings is the vainest of all philosophies. The sage, from the solitude of his chamber, speaks a loftier strain. Life, he tells us, is measured, not by minutes, but by actions. He lives well who acts well, however short be his round of days; and all too short, however long, is the life of him who has not fulfilled himself in worthy deeds. But well or ill spent, long or short, happy or miserable, at length the play is played out, and Death drops the curtain over all. If we would learn the real value of Time, we must consult, not the reasonings of men, but the teaching of Faith.

Faith, then, sets before us another measure of duration than Time, viz., that of Eternity. For, observe, that Time and Eternity do not merely differ in degree; they differ in kind. Time is one measure, and Eternity is another and different measure. In Time there is duration through change. The shadow changes on the sun-dial, the hands on the clock-face; the sun, moon and earth are changed towards each other; or, apart from these, we are still changed towards ourselves, as thought succeeds thought in our minds: hence Time. Time, then, is the measure of movement; and that it is an imperfect measure appears from this, that the measure itself is just as changeable as that which it measures. I mean, that the minutes, hours, days, or the thoughts in our minds, whereby we measure to ourselves the succession of movements, do themselves move and succeed to one another. A true and perfect measure should be somewhat steadfast and abiding; whereas, here below, all things are changed, and we ourselves are changed towards ourselves. The things of Time, we knew, were illusive; but according to this account, Time itself is equally illusion. So shall it one day be dispelled. The minute in which each one shall die shall be to each one the last minute. And again One Day (as Holy Scripture witnesses) an angel shall proclaim, with awful trumpet sound, for all flesh, that: *Time shall be no more!* and then shall begin that other order and measure of things, of which the Text speaks, wherein one day is as a thousand years, and a thousand years as one day.

And if we cannot understand *how* this can be (as surely we cannot), yet let it suffice for our instruction that, nevertheless, so it shall be. Even now, in the actual order of things, we are sometimes made aware of another measure of duration than that of Time. Thus the same period of time is long or short to different persons, accordingly as they are severally affected, or occupied in it, or to the same person, according to the circumstances in which it finds him. And if I do not merely say that it *appears* to be, but that it *is* long or short, this is because, as to matters of quantity, or duration, there is no absolute standard, but they are what they are in estimation; and just as you cannot say, in the abstract, whether or not a pound be a large sum of money, or a mile a long distance, so neither can you say if a certain given time be, in itself, long or short. Long indeed, however short, is deemed, and is, to the poor sufferer, the term of bodily torture, or mental anguish; and all the longer, as, in fretful impatience, he simply wishes it away, instead of resigning himself, and improving it to his soul's advantage. One eventful week, in like manner, is more than ordinary months; while, on the other hand, as we sometimes sadly tell ourselves, long years have sped away like so many months. There are again certain occasions, as in dreams, for instance, when Time itself seems almost annihilated, and the events or adventures of long hours are crowded into a few minutes of sleep; while persons who have been rescued from a sudden violent death sometimes tell how their whole lifetime appeared before the conscience in a single glance. Nor should such thoughts as these be set aside by any one as commonplace or trivial, if it be considered that, in spiritual matters, what is, as it were, the Alphabet, is often the most loosely learnt. Nor is that lesson less than sublime, however simple, which teaches us how we may so practically lengthen our days, as "in a short space" to "fulfil a long time," or enables us to realise, howsoever feebly, what Faith teaches of the Future State, wherein the actual order of things being abolished, there shall be no longer either Past or Future, but the same ever-enduring Present.

For such is the nature of Eternity, which is God's measure of duration. Our measure, as we have seen, is imperfect because it is changeable. A perfect measure should be unchangeable, and God is the only Unchangeable. With Him there is no flux, no succession, no vicissitude, nor "shadow of alteration;" with Him there is consequently no Time. It is not, strictly speaking, true to say of Him that He was, or that He will be, but that He *is*. To Him the Past and Future are alike present. "He calleth those things that are not as those that are." He is at once in all times, as He is at once in all places. Just as the radii of a circle are all equally present to its centre, even so are all the different points of Time equally present to His Eternity. And hence it is that in Scripture language, in which things are represented to us from God's point of view, the Past or Future oftentimes is made Present: "Amen, amen, I say unto you, before Abraham was made I *am:*"[1] "He who heareth My Word ... *hath* Everlasting Life, and *cometh* not into judgment, but *is passed* from death to life:"[2] "He that believeth in Him *is not judged*, but He that believeth not *is already judged:*"[3] "I know that His commandment *is* Everlasting Life."[4] The Eternity of God signifies, in brief, that He holds His Life, so to speak, all in all, and at once. And whereas a certain prophet of this world has spoken thus sadly, yet truly, of the goods of this world, that "All things are taken from us, and become portions and parcels of the dreadful Past," this, on the other hand, is the high and incommunicable privilege of the Almighty Creator, that He

[1] John viii. 58.   [2] Ibid. v. 24.
[3] Ibid. iii. 18.   [4] Ibid. xii. 50.

truly holds, all in all in the Present, the combined happiness of the Past and the Future. Such is the Sovereign perfection of His Blessedness, to which nothing can be added, and from which nothing can be detracted.

Now this comparison of Time with Eternity, based as it is upon the language of Holy Scripture, and the sound teaching of divines, will suggest a consideration of the greatest practical importance. When once the soul has entered within the circle of God's Eternity, it shall measure all things with His measure, to which all times are equally present. And here let me explain by a similitude:

The traveller wends his way through the changeful country: and now, suppose, the course of his journey lies along the windings of a river's margin, now through a weary expanse of heather; here he enters the noisy village street, there he is on the dusty highway; he enters a wood, he emerges again. And thus, while he keeps the level path, he only sees his journey piecemeal: as one scene appears in view, another is hidden away from the sight. But suppose now that he climb up to some lofty mountain-peak, then the whole country he has traversed in his journey is restored to the view in one scene. There again meanders the pleasant stream; here stretches the waste of heather; in yonder valley nestles the little village, and beneath his feet lies the sombre wood. And so shall it prove with the journey of life. In Time one scene succeeds to another; but in Eternity all the scenes of life shall be shown in one view. Then shall be to the wicked no Future in which to repent, but a state fixed and unalterable, and no Past, for alas! the Past is again present. The whole vista of the chequered life lies stretched out before the mind's eye. Here see again those idle, empty, unprofitable days—seasons of sowing wherein nothing has been sown save noxious weeds! Here see again those tainted moments of criminal indulgence. The soul is in Eternity, and Eternity is the vision of life all in all. Then shall there be also for the just no anxious Future, no regretful Past, no ghosts of friends departed, no songs of pensive burden, no saddened joys, no unwelcome news, no mournful farewells; but solid joys, ever-enduring delights, unfailing peace, immortal love, perfect fruition of God in all things, and all things in God.

Oh, how differently does Time appear when it is thus measured by Eternity! These years, these months, these weeks, days, hours, minutes; these sands in the glass of Time—they do not merely run out; they do not leave us as they found us; they do not begin and end with themselves (were this so the wisdom of the worldling would be justified); but our time is the womb of our eternity, and all conspire together; each is working (and how swiftly working!) to build up a life, and a life which shall endure for everlasting! Oh, how important then are those golden moments which we sometimes so recklessly squander; and if they be of such inestimable value, surely we shall be called one day to render a severe account of every idle word! How much might be done in one week, in one day—yea, in a single hour, towards building up one's self in that image, in which alone we shall bear to see ourselves in the Day of Eternity—the Image of Jesus Christ! In that day we shall truly see ourselves, and what the years have made us. And oh, if we would bear the spectacle then, let us enter now into the secret chamber of our heart, and there, tearing away every disguise of self-love, set ourself before ourself as we really are! Which of us, even now, can bear this spectacle of himself? Who does not turn away from it in pain and shame and disgust, and cry to God for mercy? What secret meanness, what narrow selfishness, what laxness of life, how much self-indulgence, how many vanities, how many sinful deeds are there presented! But yet time serves wherein we may redeem the past. Behold, another day is begun, and it finds us still alive. It brings with it new objects of interest, schemes, duties, opportunities, burdens, pleasures and pains, hopes, fears and regrets. *Carpe diem!* the maxim is sound, after all, if rightly taken. Seize the hour; make the most of it. No time like the present; for the present alone is in our power. And how make the most of it, how best employ it, but in ordering it towards that Eternity which will never cease? For the rest, the subject of Time presents to the Christian mind no occasion for complaint or regret, save only as far as our own fault is concerned. It can give us everything if we will rightly use it; while it can take nothing away which will not, at the last, be restored with interest. It may be made an inestimable blessing, while it can only hurt those who use it to their hurt.

XIV.

NEITHER COLD NOR HOT.

"I know thy works, that thou art neither cold nor hot. I would thou wert cold or hot: but because thou art lukewarm, and neither cold nor hot, I will begin to vomit thee out of my mouth. Because thou sayest, 'I am rich and made wealthy, and have need of nothing,' and knowest not that thou art wretched, and miserable, and poor, and blind, and naked: I counsel thee to buy of me gold fire-tried, that thou mayest be made rich, and mayest be clothed in white garments, and that the shame of thy nakedness may not appear; and anoint thine eyes with eye-salve, that thou mayest see. Such as I love, I rebuke and chastise. Be zealous, therefore, and do penance."
—Apoc. iii. 15-19.

SURELY the words of this text are very awful. Woe to them, it seems to say, who know not their own misery! And yet, it appears, one may be very miserable, and not know it. We may seem to stand well with God, and yet stand very ill; we may deem ourself to be an object of the divine regard, while the Almighty barely endures us, and is threatening visitation; we may seem to be rich and lacking nothing, while in His sight we are wretched, blind, and naked. For these words of rebuke, observe, are not addressed to one whom the world would call sinner, but to one who has "works,"—all the show and semblance of godliness,—a person of repute and respectability. They are addressed, in brief, to the angel, or bishop (as the word signifies in this place) of Laodicea. It most closely concerns us, then, to identify, not indeed the person, but the character here described, in order to discover if such exist in our days, and perhaps even amongst ourselves.

The opening lines of the charge have served to attach the name of lukewarm to those Christians, who, avoiding grave or scandalous sins, have yet no great zeal either for God's glory or their own spiritual advancement. This use of them is natural and suitable enough; but we narrow their meaning by separating them from the context. As they stand in Holy Scripture, they form only a portion in the delineation of a whole character. The person here described has good works, the merit of which is entirely lost because they proceed from a wrong principle. Such a one, who is on God's side, not in his heart, but only in his actions, is simply set down as inconsistent; as being neither cold nor hot; or, as we say, neither one thing nor another.

Meanwhile, his good works blind him as to his real state of spiritual destitution. He sets them down to his account; and conscience has no gross violations of the law to weigh on the other side. He would seem to have been faithful in the discharge of his pastoral duties, since there is no rebuke on that score, as there was in the case of other bishops. The reproof concerns his *spiritual state;* the state of one who is deceived by the appearance of good works. He is self-satisfied then, like the Pharisee; yet, in one respect, at least, he differs widely from the Pharisee. He is no whited sepulchre, fair to the eye, but impure and rotten within. If he deceives others as to his real character, yet this is because he deceives himself, and not because he pretends to be what he is not. His spiritual wealth is not fine gold, but counterfeit; he is not clothed with a robe of righteousness, but naked and miserable; he sees not, while he thinks he sees, but is blind to spiritual things. This is his case, and he does not know it: he would, in all likelihood, be greatly shocked to know it. Now, tribulation is the fire that tries the gold of good works, whether they be solid gold or counterfeit; and such a trial was needed in this case. The gold he is counselled to buy must be fire-tried; and the trial is sent in love: "Such as I love I rebuke and chastise. Be zealous, therefore, and do penance."

Here, then, we are taught that something else, besides good works, is necessary for salvation; but what else? This we gather from our Blessed Saviour's words to Nicodemus, when He says that "the Light is come into the world," and that "he that doth truth cometh to the Light, that his works may be made manifest, because they are done in God."[1] Works, then, *not done in God,* however good they may be in themselves, are of no profit towards

[1] John iii. 19, 21.

Eternal Life; and this is the counterfeit wealth spoken of in the text. The heresy, that good works are not necessary for salvation, was simply the corruption of this truth. Of course, they are necessary; but it is required that they be supernatural; that they be done in God: that is to say, they must be dictated by faith in God; they must be wrought by the grace of God; and they must have God for their end or object.

But I will endeavour to bring the truth home to you, brethren, by an example, which although it be not in all respects identical with the one exhibited in the text, may yet well serve to illustrate it. I will describe the character of one, out of many hundreds of persons, who would consider themselves good Christians; who would feel hurt at the imputation that they were otherwise, and yet, who would, if the truth were known, as to the secret springs and motives of their actions, well merit the rebuke of the text.

And whereas some persons have better natural dispositions than others, I will suppose one of the best possible dispositions; and again, since the best possible disposition has not always fair play, as we say, but is easily corrupted, by neglect of training, or untoward circumstances, or the force of evil example, I will further suppose, in the case of such a person as I am going to describe, the most favourable circumstances, together with the good society, and good example of others. And though I do not speak here of religious advantages, yet I will even suppose that the person under consideration has been duly instructed in the fundamental tenets of our holy Religion; so that, whatever fault there be is not owing to his teachers, or associates, but simply to himself.

Well: the result at length answers to the most sanguine expectations. A merry, light-hearted, but strictly dutiful, and well-disposed youth, at length grows into the prime of manhood. His early promise has been amply fulfilled, and so far as our common infirmity will allow (for it is not human to be perfect, even according to the lowest standard of excellence), he is all that the world can expect in a man—an ideal, if you will, of human excellence; honest, straightforward, candid, truthful, thoroughly courteous, and refined; an agreeable companion; fair and reasonable even towards his enemies. He never seems to think of himself, but is all consideration for others. He confers a favour with such a grace, it would almost seem it was himself who was under obligation. He is careful never to wound another's feelings, in word or deed; and has an admirable tact in conciliating others; a result of his knowledge of the world, and of human nature. And, finally, he is a very charitable man, but without ostentation in his benevolence.

Now some of these qualities, it is true, are such as a man might assume to gain his own private ends; but with him, at least, this is not the case. His character is genuine, and his motives sincere. He wishes to deal fairly and rightly with others, because he loves what is fair and right; and not because honesty is the best policy. He is kind and courteous, for kindliness' and courteousness' sake; because he is naturally of a benevolent and humane disposition; and because his early training has all tended to foster in him this disposition, and to repress its contrary. He is, in short, naturally good; and consequently naturally averse to evil. And if from time to time, by the sudden surprise of temptation, or the sheer violence of passion, he is betrayed into evil-doing of whatsoever kind, yet it is no exaggeration to say that he hates himself for it; and is heartily ashamed of it. Nay he is cut to the quick, and hurt beyond measure; because he feels that he has behaved unworthily of himself, and of that standard of excellence which it has been the business of his life to cultivate in himself. He may even consider that sin is an offence against God (for remember, we are contemplating the case of a Christian); but what he chiefly considers is, that it is an offence against decorum and good-breeding; that to be the slave of passion is unworthy of a man, and still more unworthy of a gentleman.

And from a similar motive he respects his religion and its ministers, and conforms himself to its various obligations; for he would despise himself, if he professed one thing with his lips, and practised another in his life. That he also faithfully discharges the duties of his domestic and social life need scarcely be added; that he is a good husband, a good father, a loyal soldier, a conscientious physician, an equitable magistrate; as the case may be. Throughout his character is of a piece; it is consistent, and harmonious; and, at least outwardly, will bear the closest scrutiny.

And what more would you have? you may ask me, brethren. What more would you expect in a man? Wherein is he not justified? He is not a saint, it is true; for a saint belongs to another order of things; but he does his duty; and for a man of the world, and a true Christian gentleman, what more does he want, that he is not perfect?

Well then, brethren, I will tell you what he wants. What he wants is *Grace;* what he wants is the Spirit. For in all this, how does his justice exceed that of the heathen? He is of the flesh, as the Scripture phrases it; and "that which is born of the flesh is flesh, and that which is born of the Spirit is spirit."[1] In all his thoughts, words and works, he is merely human, and "flesh and blood," however clean and refined, cannot "possess the kingdom of God."[2] He does his duty, you say; true, according to the *letter*, and has kept the commandments from his youth upwards, but how as to the *spirit* of the commandments? "Thou shalt love the Lord thy God with thy whole heart, with thy whole soul, and with thy whole mind; and with thy whole strength ... and thy neighbour as thyself."[3] Oh, my brethren, be not deceived. To be true and just towards men, faithful to one's engagements, good husbands, and fathers of families, and correct in all the social relations of life—this is within the power of unrenewed

[1] John iii. 6. [2] 1 Cor. xv. 50. [3] Mark xii. 30.

nature; these things the heathens do; but to be fashioned in the image of Jesus Christ, this is a divine gift which cometh down from the Father of Lights.

That the grace of God is necessary for salvation, he had heard, of whom I speak; he had only forgotten it. Or indeed, perhaps from the first, he had never thoroughly learnt the lesson; he never quite realised it. Perhaps (the case is quite possible) he had misunderstood what was said. That a man cannot think so much as a good thought, in order to salvation, that "no man can say the Lord Jesus, but in the Holy Ghost"—this indeed he had always believed. He had understood well enough that we depend upon God to live so as to live well, and work justice and goodness; just as we depend upon Him and His providence for the food we eat, and the air we breathe (for so he misexplains the doctrine in his own mind),—just as even the brute beasts depend upon Him, which also, like ourselves, live and move in Him, and have their being. And so he erred as to the very notion of divine grace; viewing it as a mere natural gift of God, instead of what it really is, a gift over and above nature, designed to new-create us in Jesus Christ, and lift us out of the misery and depravity of nature.

Or else, if he rightly thought upon the subject of grace, yet he does not realise the doctrine in his life and actions. He does not live according to grace, but according to nature. It is true he says his prayers, night and morning,—rather perhaps through habit than any real sense of what is due to God, or what is wanting in himself. Throughout the day, he hardly thinks of God, or speaks to Him. He does not live for God, or He puts Him in a very poor, second place. He lives and works for himself, for his fellow-men, and for the world. And verily he has his reward; he is saluted in the streets and high places; he is beloved, honoured, almost revered; and he feels that he deserves it. His own conscience seems to reflect the applause of the crowd. He enters the church of God on the Sunday, or festival, with firm step, and head erect, and bold front, and complacent smile; but in the judgment of God the heart-broken child of sin and shame is justified rather than he.

And now, if God would win this soul to Himself, there is only the way of tribulation. How else should a man be taught that he is not sufficient for himself, but by being put to the proof? Hitherto, perhaps, he had no real sense of the natural misery of humanity. He had entertained no lofty spiritual aspirations of any kind, and therefore knew not the more than leaden weight of flesh and blood. He would scarcely understand the Apostle's lament over the conflict of "the spirit" with "this body of death," or his desire "to be dissolved and be with Christ." He had had, as a rule, no considerable temptations; his worldly affairs had prospered; he had always enjoyed good health and spirits, and was blessed with an equable temperament; and, on the whole, all things had run so smoothly well with him, that excepting such troubles of daily life as are common to all men, he has hardly known so much as what affliction is.

Such is his state, and it is a conceivable state; but that it should endure for any considerable period of time is certainly not conceivable. For merely natural virtue cannot stand in the season of temptation or adversity. And he must, for his soul's health, be at length rudely awakened from his dream of security; and either by domestic affliction, or some, humanly speaking, insuperable temptation, or by heavy pecuniary losses, or whatsoever other calamity, be brought (if haply so it prove) to acknowledge hi sown insufficiency, and to cry to God, at last, for that help of which he never before owned the necessity.

The blow falls and he is crushed. He looks to the right hand and to the left; but there is no help for it, and he finds none in himself. The visitation of God searches him like the fire. At first, he would harden his heart, he would wrap himself up in his pride, he would set his face like brass against the onset. But in vain. He only writhes, like the worm that is trodden on by the heel. At last his spirit is broken, and he bows, he yields, he *despairs*. But it is a saving despair; for it is not of God he despairs (he had not thought of God), but of *himself;* and despairing of himself, now, for the first time, he thinks of God. He cries to Him in the agony of his soul. They are no longer tears of wounded pride that he is shedding now (he has, at least, unlearned pride), but genuine tears. And with his tears ascends before God that prayer of a contrite and humbled heart which He will never despise. The Almighty, the Lord of mercies, inclines and hearkens; and His grace descends into the heart. And the grace of God, while it soothes and comforts and strengthens, is an eye-salve to the spirit. The scales are fallen from his eyes. He sees it all now: his whole life was a delusion. He had deceived himself; he had deceived others; he had only the show, and not the substance of godliness: his virtues were merely worldly, heathen virtues; his works were not wrought in God, but in *self*. He had built upon a wrong foundation, and all had to be done over again. But just now it is, when he owns himself wretched and miserable, and poor and blind and naked, that God will assist, and clothe, and enlighten, and enrich him, according to the loving purpose of His visitation.

It may perhaps be asked, How does this example concern ourselves? Is it possible that duly instructed Catholics, such as we are, should be ignorant of so essential a truth as that of man's natural misery and nothingness, and the consequent necessity of divine grace? But the question is, (about which I would have each one consult his own heart), whether he not only believes, but realises, and acts upon the truth, in the conduct of daily life? Is it in God, or in ourselves, that we trust, in times of trouble, or difficulty, or affliction, or temptation? And here I do not deny that there is a sense in which we may, and must, trust also in ourselves.

Vain were even the grace of God without our own co-operation. But that we should overlook our own part, I think, is the lesser danger: do we also remember God's part? Do we frequently think of Him, speak to Him, refer our actions to Him, ask His help? Our works, are they done in God, or in self? For, alas! so inconsistent are we that, while we readily own the one foundation, yet we build on the other. We believe in grace, but we trust in ourselves; what wonder then if we fall short?

And oh, my brethren, examine well if this be your case; for, if it be, I am assured that a time of severest trial is at hand! Be sure that shortly God will search you in the fire of tribulation and prove what spirit you are of. In pain and sorrow, in affliction, or temptation, or humiliation; in one way or another, He will find you out, and reveal all your spiritual nakedness. He will make you know what you are. And need I say, that far better for your own everlasting welfare that He so prove you? For self-sufficiency there is no other remedy than the fire. Ah, when you have tasted somewhat of the cup of woe and wretchedness, then you will learn, perforce, to lean upon God, and find in Him your last rest and sovereign happiness! For what the Apostle says of the visitation at the Last Day, is true of every visitation in this life, that, "Other foundation no man can lay but that which is laid, which is Christ Jesus. Now, if any man build upon this foundation gold, silver, precious stones, wood, hay, stubble, every man's work shall be manifest; for the day of the

Lord shall declare it, because it shall be revealed in fire. And the fire shall try every man's work, of what sort it is. If any man's work abide, which he hath built thereon, he shall receive a reward. If any man's work burn, he shall suffer loss: but he himself shall be saved, yet so as by fire."[1]

[1] 1 Cor. iii. 11, *et seq.*

XV.

SPECULATIVE PIETY.

"Be ye doers of the word, and not hearers only, deceiving your own selves. For if a man be a hearer of the word, and not a doer, he shall be compared to a man beholding his own countenance in a glass: for he beheld himself, and went his way, and presently forgot what manner of man he was."—St. James i. 22-24.

ST. JAMES, in describing the case of those who are hearers only, and not doers of the word, notices, by way of illustration, the fact, which would be remarkable were it less familiar than it is, that no man truly knows his own face. For a moment, before the glass, he sees himself as he really is; but when he turns away, the image, which the mirror had faithfully reflected, refuses to be imprinted on the memory. The reason is not far to seek. Our natural self-love, which cannot be satisfied with the reality that we are, induces in us a powerful tendency to idealise. But, in like manner, as the illustration imports, neither does a man quite know the face of his soul, that is to say, his own natural character; and for the same reason. Our faults may be as gross as mountains in the eyes of our neighbour, but they sit too closely near to our heart of flesh, with its concupiscences, for us either to see them in their true light or to hate them, as they are seen and hated by the rest of the world. And as the same prompting of self-love which endears to ourselves our vices also enhances and glorifies our virtues, it comes about that, when the mind's eye looks inward on itself, what meets its gaze is rather an ideal than our real self: it is indeed our portrait, but the artist, so to speak, has flattered us; and we see in this likeness, not so much what we are, as what God intended us to be. And here the ministry of the Word comes most opportunely to our service; for it strips away the disguise, and, like the mirror, shows us ourselves as we truly are in God's sight; and that in a manner, as I will presently show, which forbids our self-love to creep in and mar the effect of the lesson.

But in order thoroughly to enter into the Apostle's drift, and because the ministry of the Word is very various, let us see, in the first place, what sort of sermon St. James must have had in his mind, when he wrote the words of the text; for St. Paul, in his first epistle to the Corinthians, enumerates several kinds of sermons. Of those who address the congregation, he tells us, that to one is given the "word of wisdom," to another the "word of knowledge," and to another the gift of "tongues;" but there is another kind of preaching which St. Paul mentions, and on which he himself sets chief store; and that is the gift of "prophecy."[1] I must here observe, however, that the word prophecy has somewhat altered its meaning in modern times; it is used by us in a narrower sense than that in which the Apostle used it. A prophet, in the original meaning of the word, was not merely one who foretold things to come, but one who spoke to man in behalf of God—a messenger, in short, from God to man; whether the subject of his message regarded the present, or the future disposition of events. In this sense, the Christian preacher exactly fulfils the office of the prophets of old. And that this was the sense in which St. Paul speaks of the prophetical discourse seems clear from the manner in which he describes it. "He that prophesieth," he says, "speaketh to men unto edification, and exhortation, and comfort;" and that, "if all prophesy, and there come in an unbeliever, or an unlearned person, he is convinced of all, he is judged of all. The secrets of his heart are made manifest; and so, falling down on his face, he will adore God, affirming that God is among you indeed."[2] The preacher has held up the mirror to his soul's face, and thus manifested to him the secrets of his heart. And this also, no doubt, is the kind of sermon to which St. James alludes, when he tells us, in the words of the text, that, "if a man be a hearer of the word, and not a doer, he shall be compared to a man beholding his own face in a glass; for he beheld himself, and went his way, and presently forgot what manner of man he was." And what, in the prophetical

---

[1] 1 Cor. xii. 8, *et seq.*   [2] Ibid. xiv. 3, 23.

discourse, answers to the glass is the parable, or similitude, which was a distinctive feature in the teaching of the prophets of old, as it is also in the teaching of Him whom the prophets foretold—our Blessed Saviour, whose parables are read to us in the Gospel, Sunday after Sunday. These are instances in point: they hold up to the soul a mirror, but of such a virtue that it shows a man his face, *as if it were that of another person;* and thus self-love is forestalled, which else might intrude to warp the judgment, until the preacher, in expounding the parable and applying the moral of its story, says to him in effect: "*Thou art the man!*"

But enough on this head, since it is not my present purpose to insist on the excellency of this kind of teaching, but rather to determine what is the special danger which the Apostle warns us against, on receiving the "Word," viz., that of contenting ourselves with what I will call a merely *Speculative Piety*. I mean that, just as there are certain sciences which are called speculative, as opposed to practical, because they are cultivated, not for any useful purpose, but for the knowledge sake, and the pleasurable excitement which attends its pursuit, and the mental enlargement which results from it; even so, religious knowledge may become to us (if we will perversely so make it) not indeed a matter of awful practical moment, which it is, but an end in itself, and cultivated merely for its own interest, and the emotional gratification which belongs to it. And the false piety engendered of such a knowledge, which never passes from contemplation into action, may suitably be called speculative, since *speculum* (from which the word is derived) signifies a looking-glass. The preacher holds up the mirror of the Word, and the man sees his face; but he is none the better, or he is rather, in one way, the worse for it, since he perverts the Word to his own delusion, *deceiving his own self;* and he will go away, and presently forget what manner of man he was.

And lest any one should think this point overstrained (though I cannot think I am exceeding the scope of the text), yet consider the case of the dramatist. There is nothing unworthy in the comparison; for although corrupted oftentimes, as everything human is liable to be corrupted, the drama is, in its own nature, noble and elevating; and there are points, both of contact and contrast, between a drama and a sermon which it may prove instructive to consider. The dramatic poet then, I say, commends his art (it is not a little remarkable that he so commends it) in the very same terms as the Apostle. He, too, declares that he *holds up the mirror unto nature,* shows Virtue her own feature, Scorn her image, and the Age its fashion and impression; but would any one suppose for a moment that either the poet himself, or the gifted mimic who renders his ideals on the stage, must therefore practise in actual life (he *may* do so, of course) those heroic virtues which move the plaudits of his audience, or that the audience who have applauded must needs go and do likewise? Were it not childish to expect this? But you will remind me that there is always this vast difference between the best of dramas and a sermon, that the former offers us something to *admire* only, while the latter proposes something for us *to do*. Exactly: and that is the very point that I wish to insist upon; that many persons think they are virtuous merely because they are affected with virtuous emotions, or approve virtuous deeds; whereas they would be simply inhuman did they not so feel and admire. Who doubts but that the actor in the drama really feels, for the moment, the virtuous emotions which he expresses? When he weeps over Hecuba his tears are *real*, though Hecuba herself be a fiction. It is to this he owes his very art, that whatsoever character he assumes, his fancy has so wrought upon him he really burns with the righteous indignation, withering scorn, or maddening remorse, or whatsoever other passion he affects, and so is enabled to act it to the very life. And his audience—they feel with him: it is the very luxury of emotions that are amongst the finest and noblest in our nature, which is the object of the exhibition.

And thus does the drama hold up the mirror unto nature: but beyond the mere interest of the spectacle itself, and the virtuous emotions excited by it (for I am speaking always of such dramas as are virtuous; it is only too notorious that many of them are just the reverse), observe, that nothing further, ordinarily speaking, comes of it. The curtain falls, and the spectators come away, and shortly forget all about it in the din and turmoil of real life. And he who had just now been moved, wellnigh to tears perhaps at a fictitious distress, may turn his back on the first real object of compassion that crosses his path; while the fellow who had so lustily applauded the honest man in the play is presently convicted of theft; and he who had laughed at the prodigal goes his way, and, on the first occasion, himself acts the spendthrift: and so of the rest. The man has seen his face; but as it neither makes nor mars a face to see itself reflected in the glass, so he leaves the house of entertainment just the same as he went into it.

Now, although the sacred preacher and the dramatic poet use the same similitude in characterising their respective arts, yet it need hardly be said that, apart from what the similitude itself suggests that they have in common, there is almost every other difference between a sermon and a drama. It is not merely that the theme of the former is sacred and heavenly, while that of the latter is worldly and profane—oftentimes in the worst sense of the word; or that the one holds up a divine Model and the other exhibits the deeds of mere human heroes; or that the former treats of awful realities, while the latter deals with fiction, or fact so rendered as to be little better than fiction; but, as we have seen, the very scope and aim of the two arts is different. The drama is a mere spectacle which begins and ends with itself. We have only to sit still, with folded arms, and admire and wonder, and laugh and weep by turns: that is all. We need not gird up our loins, for there is nothing for us *to do*, seeing that the whole thing is a fiction. But the preacher, on the other hand, is practical, or he is nothing: "Be ye doers of the word" must ever be his motto, or he is only a "sounding brass or a tinkling cymbal." Still if, as we have seen in the instance of the drama, righteous feeling may be quite divorced from righteous doing, why, in spite of the practical aim of the preacher (since so much depends also on the disposition of the audience), may not the same be the case with a sermon? But indeed is it not the very meaning of the text that it is commonly the case? And the way in which it comes to be so, I think, is thus:

While the dramatist, as we have just now seen, sets before us a world of fancies, in order to excite in us a flow of fine generous feelings which, ordinarily speaking, lead to nothing beyond themselves, and the mere luxury of indulging them, the preacher, on the other hand, treats of such momentous realities as God, our Maker and our Judge; the fallen condition of our race, and its restoration to the divine Sonship through the redemption of Jesus Christ; the meaning and purpose of life; and the Resurrection and Afterlife beyond the grave. These, since they purport to be *facts*, must, as such, when proclaimed with fitting earnestness, induce in us the most forcible incentives to action; since, these things being so, a man must be a fool to lead a godless, sinful life, which can only end, if he persist in it, in his own everlasting undoing. But now mark what follows upon this—viz., that if, when such truths as these are set before us, we refuse to act upon them, we are *practically* treating them as fictions; we are behaving as though they were untrue: and the result will surely be (such a habit of mind will be induced in us by our neglect) that, at last, they will become to us as nothing better than fictions. I do not mean to say, indeed, that we shall end in thinking they are untrue; yet, if we never act upon them, they might just as well be untrue for any advantage that will accrue to ourselves from them. Neither do I mean that we shall cease to care for them, or dislike to hear about them (such effect might indeed follow upon our neglect, but it *need* not); nor, lastly, do I mean that they will cease to awe, or melt, or soothe, or sober, or terrify us, at least for the time being; for do not the fictions of the drama likewise produce such effects for the time being on the susceptible audience? And so the solemn truths of religion may still powerfully affect our feelings, though practically we regard them as fictions; but alas! what good will that do us if nothing, after all, ever comes of these fine feelings— if we never proceed to realise them in action? Nay, so far from doing us any good, the idle indulgence of such feelings may work us positive harm; since, as it has been finely remarked by a devout thinker, "God has made us feel, in order that we may go on to *act* in consequence of feeling. If, then, we allow our feelings to be excited without acting upon them, we do mischief to the moral system within us, just as we might spoil a watch, or other piece of mechanism, by playing with the wheels of it."[1]

[1] Newman: "Parochial Sermons," vol. ii. Serm. xxx.

But the result, on the whole, of neglecting to act on our religious feelings is to beget in a man the mischievous delusion that he is devout, simply because he is, so to speak, educated in religious sentiments, and keenly susceptible to spiritual emotions; though his practice be never so meagre and wretched. Such a person will frequent the church on the Sunday or festival, and not merely out of human respect; a sense of his own need urges him, and the horror of living "without God in the world." For the sentiment of religious awe is natural to the heart of man; and he would feel uneasy in his mind, not to say wretched, if he stayed at home, or walked in the fields instead. And so he comes: and once in the church, the very holiness of the place, the devout attitude of the worshippers, the fragrance of prayer and praise around him—all these incentives stimulate his natural feelings of devotion; and he tells himself that it is indeed "good for us to be here." And then, when the man of God, in the "glass" of his discourse, shows him his soul's face, he listens with attention and interest, and, it may be, takes what is said straight home to himself. *Thou art the man*, the preacher has said to him, as plainly as if he had singled out himself alone from the midst of the congregation. It is thou to whom the Lord forgave the vast debt of ten thousand talents, and thou hast throttled thy fellow-servant over a hundred pence; or thou, that didst pass by, with the priest and levite, unconcerned, while thy neighbour lay robbed and bleeding by the wayside; or thou, that wouldst thrust thyself, thy rags and filth, into the nuptial circle of the Lamb, not having on thee a wedding-garment. Thus urged, I say, on one indictment or another, he pleads guilty, he humbles himself, and is confounded: nay, he prays; and like the publican, "Lord," he says, "be merciful unto me a sinner!" All this may be, and yet he will not obtain mercy; and why? Simply because his heart is unchanged. For although, suppose, he has committed injustices in the past, he does not intend to restore the ill-gotten gain; or, although he lives under the control of some fatal passion, yet he cannot resolve to break with that; and although he is without the pale of the Church, yet he will not seek the sacrament of reconciliation. To what end, then, you may ask, are his religious observance, his conviction of sin, his confusion of face, his ineffectual prayers, or even tears? They are their own end. This is his religion, which, never forget, the Apostle says, "is vain." It is for this purpose he is here: it has been a relief to him; it has been almost like a balm to his soul's wounds, thus to be awed and humbled in the presence of God, and thus probed and searched by His minister. It has been thus with him before, and it will be thus again: for although "the fear of the Lord is the beginning of wisdom," yet it is only the beginning; and such as he never get beyond the beginning. For a short space, he has beheld himself in God's light, but he will straightway go and forget what manner of man he was. His neighbours, seeing that his practice is still and ever unchanged, may call him hypocrite: but why? He never, it is likely, either feigned to be what he was not, or dissembled what he was. No: he is not a hypocrite; he is simply one of those who say, "Lord, Lord!" and of whom it is written: "Not every one that saith to Me, 'Lord, Lord!' shall enter into the Kingdom of Heaven; but he that doeth the will of My Father who is in Heaven, he shall enter into the Kingdom of Heaven."[1] Scoffers will say that his case is just an instance of what themselves have always maintained; that it plainly shows that men are not one whit the better for religious observances; whereas it only shows that no religious observances are effectual without a *good will;* and, in fact, only "to men of good will" was the peace of the Gospel first proclaimed, and only to such is it ever given to enter into its blessedness.

This then, on the whole, seems to be the lesson of the text (and we ought not to despise it because it is a very simple one), that it is not enough to hear the word with attention and emotion, unless (which is quite another thing) we are also prepared to practise it. Nor should it much surprise us if one who has devoutly listened to the sermon in the morning should belie it by his conduct in the evening, or even if the preacher himself should sometimes fall short of the lofty standard which, as in duty bound, he has upheld to the congregation. The sermon, to pastor and people alike, serves only as a *rule* whereby to measure their own crookedness—I mean that, of it-

[1] Matt. vii. 25.

self, it is no more than this: it is only more, as we ourselves make it more, "who, in a good and perfect heart, hearing the word keep it, and bring forth fruit in patience."[1]—A simple truth, I say, and yet one which it is well worth while to insist upon, when we consider the numbers of persons who build up the last hope of their eternal welfare on the mere profession of that faith which they have denied in their lives, who "detain the truth of God in injustice;"[2] and whose best plea for themselves is, to use their own language, that, "after all, their heart is in the right place"—which means, forsooth, that they love, admire, and revere that good which they are too faint-hearted, or too indolent, or too self-indulgent to practise! And they trust an All-just, All-holy God will vouchsafe to accept the service of their barren professions, and overlook their corrupt practices!

Oh, what will it avail, when the awful day of reckoning shall come, to fill the mouth with smooth words, if the hands be empty of good works? or what avail to cry for mercy when the hour of mercy is past and the hour of justice is begun; when the day is spent and "the night cometh wherein no man can work?" The priest had read over the dying man, "Remember, O Lord, that he is Thy creature;" that, "although he has sinned, yet he has always firmly believed in the Father, the Son, and the Holy Ghost; he has had a zeal for Thine honour, and faithfully adored Thee as his God and the Creator of all things:" but what says the Judge? "I never

[1] Luke viii. 15. [2] Rom. i. 18.

knew ye: depart from Me, all ye workers of iniquity."[1]

In conclusion, my brethren, let us diligently examine ourselves as to how far it is true that we are hearers only of the Word, and not doers. Let us resolve to measure ourselves henceforth, no longer by our professions, or our aspirations, or our devotional feelings, or even our good resolutions, but solely by the faithfulness of our practice. And as an earnest that we are serious, let us start at once. If there be something to be undone or amended in the past, let us first look to that; if we have entangled ourselves in the meshes of evil habit, or sustain the onset of some present ruling passion, let us begin with that. Let that day be accounted as loss to us which has been marked by no result towards our spiritual advancement. So when the Lord shall come to prove our work by fire, may we deserve to hear, instead of a sentence of condemnation, the glad welcome, "Well done, thou good and faithful servant: because thou hast been faithful over a few things, I will make thee ruler over many things: enter into the joy of thy Lord."[2]

[1] Matt. vii. 23; Luke xiii. 27.   [2] Matt. xxv. 23.

XVI.

THE GLORY OF GOD.

"I shall be satisfied when Thy Glory shall appear."—Ps. xvi. 15.

AS though the Psalmist should say: "There is something, nay, there is much in this fair world, O Lord God, which speaks to us of Thy Glory; but, alas! it disappoints, because it only provokes the desire of Thee which it does not satisfy; and it is never enough for us until Thou show us, no longer its troubled reflection, but the Glory Itself, which is Thyself!"

Now the Glory of the Lord, which is the object of the Psalmist's desire, is surely His Beauty. For only consider (unless the matter be obvious enough without such consideration) how very frequently the notions of glory and beauty are conjoined in Holy Scripture. Thus we read that the Lord appointed "a holy vesture" to be made for Aaron "for *glory* and for *beauty*."[1] Again, when the Ark of the Covenant was brought from the house of Obededom into

[1] Ex. xxviii. 2.

the city of David, it is said that the singers sang before it, "Give ye unto the Lord *glory* to His Name . . . adore the Lord in holy *comeliness*."[1] And the Psalmist, in like manner, sings, "I have loved, O Lord, the *beauty* of Thy House, and the place where Thy *Glory* dwelleth."[2] And to the same purpose, the "fading flower," as the emblem of perishable beautifulness, is called by the prophet Isaias "the *glory* of Ephraim's joy;"[3] and our Lord tells us in the Gospel that "not even Solomon, in all his *glory*, was arrayed as the lilies of the field."[4] Such texts as these, which might be almost indefinitely multiplied, would seem to indicate either that the Glory of God and His Beauty are identical, or else, if a distinction has to be made, that His Glory is, as it were, but the smile and radiance of His Beauty. And if our Blessed Saviour speaks repeatedly of His Passion as His Glory, though it left in Him "no beauty nor comeliness,"[5] this is obviously because it was through His Sacred Passion that He entered into His Glory; and if the manner of it was uncomely, yet, in the supreme exaltation of the beauty of holiness, how comely was that uncomeliness!

The Glory of God, then, is His Beauty; and it is a primary note of insufficiency, on the part of creatures, that this Glory is reflected in them, as it were, piece-meal, in broken splendours, from the very necessity of the case, since the finite must always be inadequate to express the Infinite. Our bodily

---

[1] 1 Paral. xvi. 29. [2] Ps. xxv. 8. [3] Isa. xxviii. 1.
[4] Matt. vi. 29. [5] Isa. liii. 2.

senses, through which, as windows, His brightness is shed in upon the soul, divide, while they reveal Him; as do also the objects themselves which we perceive by means of them. As one flower takes from the sunbeam one hue, another another, even so do all creatures divide amongst themselves the reflection of His attributes; and yet, so far from combining to express Him, one kind of beauty is essentially exclusive of another, and there is no perfect symbol of God, in nature. "One is the glory of the sun, another the glory of the moon, and another the glory of the stars;" and "star differeth from star in glory;"[1] and flower cannot vie with flower; for the meanest that blows has some special charm, in pattern, or colour, or perfume, which belongs to itself alone, and to no other. And hence the attainment of one excellence is commonly the death of another. Strains of concerted music are composed which search the heart as the natural songs of birds can never do; but the latter are brighter and more joyous; nor do they haunt the soul, or ever pall upon the ear, like the artificial sweetness of lutes and viols. So the fresh-budding rose has an attraction all its own, which is lost when the flower is blown; the virgin grace of morning dies before the larger light of day; and the child ripens into youth or maiden, only at the cost of that darling delight which had endeared it to us as child. In like manner the seasons of the year have each their respective charms, which exclude one another; and all things

---

[1] 1 Cor. xv. 41.

change and pass: though, even were they steadfast, yet ourselves are changed; and our day of joy returns, but it is another joy.

Now there would be something almost saddening in this aspect of our mortal condition, if there were not given to us, as Christians, some well-grounded hope that our past happiness should, in substance, be restored to us; that we should recover, hereafter, if not every object that we had tenderly loved on earth, yet all that was really worthy of our affection, or that we ever truly loved in it. Indeed it would seem that their Creator had impressed upon the very nature of the nobler delights of life certain hints and tokens to the effect that their joy does not quite die with themselves; is not altogether lost, though awhile it is withheld from us, but is as if kept in store, and shall, one day (if we be found faithful), be renewed in us. Can any man explain, else, how it is that such a mere trifle as the song of a bird, or the scent of a flower, will sometimes awaken in the heart (but with a keenness and volume which should be felt, rather than described) some long-forgotten bliss of childhood? Or can the subtler power of musical harmonies, to recall some far-off, mysterious happiness in the past, be accounted for by the throbbings of strings, or vibrations of the air, or the vulgar link of associations? And what is thus insinuated, in nature, is, in Holy Scripture, openly proclaimed; since it speaks of the Future Glory as being inaugurated by a renovation of the natural world. "For the expectation of the creature," writes

St. Paul, "waiteth for the revelation of the sons of God ... because the creature also itself shall be delivered from the servitude of corruption into the liberty of the Glory of the children of God."[1] And to the same effect our heavenly Abode is described, in the Apocalypse, as a restoration of the earthly Paradise, with its "River of Life, clear as crystal, going forth from the Throne of God and the Lamb," and the "Tree of Life," bearing its immortal leaves, "for the healing of the nations;" and we read: "Behold, I make all things new."[2]

But apart from such considerations as these, there is one sense in which we may rest assured that no slightest spark or hue of beauty ever really perishes: it abides in its Source, which is God. For He is the Origin, and the Reason, and the Law of all things that are beautiful; He is that infinite Ocean of Beauty, from which all the manifold and various perfections of creatures are derived; and in which they co-exist, in an eminent manner, unalloyed, without division, contradiction, exclusion, change, decay, or loss: *I shall be satisfied when Thy Glory shall appear.*

Another note of insufficiency, in the actual condition of created beauty, is its "vanity," or unreality. But I do not mean that it is unreal, merely because it has no lasting abidance, except, as I have just now said, with God; but because, even while it lasts, it is nothing that we can really grasp, or appropriate. We call the beauty of the rainbow unreal, not only for the reason that its colours are evanescent, but

---

[1] Rom. viii. 19, 21.   [2] Apoc. xxii. 1, 2; xxi. 5.

because its seemingly solid, burnished arc eludes our contact, in unsubstantial mists and rains. And the beauty of the rainbow is the type of all earthly beauty. Those grand hills which, in the distance, had presented to the traveller so fairy-like a prospect, their summits bathed in the golden light of morning, become disenchanted at once, when he nears the barren mountain side. The scene is a vision of glory, but that is all; it has no more reality than has the rainbow: and there is nothing of all this wealth of form and colour and radiance, that we can really make our own, save only its memory which we pensively cherish. And the same remark holds good also as to beauty in that aspect which wins us most, of human form and feature: it is unreal, not merely because it fades with lapse of time, but indeed it can hardly be said, even while it lasts, to belong to the mortal body, since it has not subsistence in itself, but is a mere reflection of the hidden beauty of the soul. For it is the soul of a man, rather than his body, which is himself, and which we truly love in wife, or child, or friend, or brother. And it is the soul which, under God, is the source of beauty to the body. There is no speculation in the eye, no charm of hue or lustre on brow or cheek, no rippling smile on the lip, or fire of eloquence on the tongue, but owes its origin to "the spirit which quickeneth" within; and "the flesh profiteth nothing" save only as it may furnish an apter medium whereby to render the subtle graces of the soul. And yet the soul itself we can neither see nor touch, nor perceive by means of any of the senses. Though near to us, it is as if afar off: the closest embrace is void; we only clasp the dust and ashes. And so all earthly beauty, the highest as the lowest, is unreal; and "the eye is not satisfied with seeing, nor the ear filled with hearing," because we are never confronted with the substance of the Good and Fair, but are merely suffered to contemplate its unenduring semblance and reflection: *I shall be satisfied when Thy Glory shall appear.*

And yet there is a reality in this unreality of earthly beauty, and that in the very respect which makes it goodly seeming in our eyes; but it is to be sought, not in the fair creation itself, which is rent or crushed, or withers and perishes, but in Him who conceived it in His infinite Mind and fashioned it. For it is not the material object itself, compact of finer clay (the finest as the coarsest is only dust and ashes); it is God's art in it that compels our admiration and provokes our love; and take away, from bird, or flower, or face, or scene so witching fair, that ideal or pattern which is His Thought in it, and nought of it remains that can longer claim of us a care or a sigh. And again this pattern, howsoever exquisitely designed, and further enhanced, in brilliant lustre, dainty colouring, or sweet perfume, moves our regard, not so much by what it is in itself, as by what it suggests to us of the character (to use an unequal word) of its divine Author; just as a human face attracts us, not so much by cold beauty of outline, as by expression. Thus, beautiful as is the unruffled expanse of ocean, it is as the mirror of His infinitude that it rivets the gaze, and feasts our soul through the eye; the sun in its meridian brightness, which blinds with excess of light, speaks to us of that Glory of His Face which no man can behold and live; the stars in their sparkling profusion are eloquent of the inexhaustible wealth and resources of the splendours of His Heavenly Kingdom; the huge mountain walls that seem to touch the roof of Heaven tell of His Almighty Power and Stability: and what were the flowers of the earth—silly gauds, childhood's frail playthings—but for "the thoughts too deep for tears" that they move in us of His splendid Magnificence, stainless Purity, faultless Perfection, touching Condescension, witching Grace, fatherly Providence, tender Solicitude and Love? Or what were the songs of birds—mere warbling prettinesses—save for the meaning of their melody, when the grove is as a choir, and the lark spurns the flowery mead and young and mate, and through and above the summer clouds, into the white light of heaven, flutters with panting raptures up to God? or the nightingale, wakeful with love and joy, "prevents the sun" to chant His praises?

And thus, vain, unenduring, unreal in itself, the glory of creation is solid, abiding, substantial, love-worthy, in God, and in Him alone. Let us then, brethren, love and enjoy the fair creations of God—if only we know how to estimate them at their real worth; if we have realised that their transient comeliness is but as it were a sunbeam fallen on them from

His Face; if, in loving them, we feel that we are learning all the better to love Him; if we can forego them at once, so soon as we perceive that, through our own weakness, their very goodliness is become a risk of stumbling; and if we do not place in them our last rest and satisfaction: else we lean on a broken reed. They cannot stand to us in His stead; they are but as types and foretokens of His Glory— a promise, rather than a possession: *I shall be satisfied when Thy Glory shall appear.*

A third note of insufficiency in the beauty of created objects is its illusion; but of course the source of this illusion lies, not with themselves, but with man's own disordered spirit. Their beauty, for as much as it is of divine origin, ought not indeed to prove a scandal of offence in our path; but, alas! out of the malice and perverseness of sin-tainted nature, so it is; and the idolatry of the creature is at the root of all evil. For in the same manner that men pride themselves on their health or wealth or stature or talents, as though such qualities were really something of their own, and not the pure gift of God's bounty towards them, even so do they ascribe the several gifts and graces of other creatures to the creatures themselves, instead of the All-fair Creator who is revealed in them. And, then, oh stupendous infatuation! this fair canopy of heaven, and green, flowery earth, with all the divine show and pageantry of nature, which, to childhood's blameless gaze, the Glory of God most transparently shone through, become as walls of adamant to block Him out. The creature grows huge in import, and arrayed in the robe of His adornment, which now purports to be its own proper quality, it usurps His place, and aspires to fill the heart of man,—if aught but He could ever fill it, if aught but He could ever assuage its immortal craving. Then is fulfilled that which the Lord complained by the mouth of the prophet Ezechiel, under the similitude of a faithless spouse who had turned the gift of His precious raiment upon her to His own despite and dishonour: "*I* clothed thee with embroidery," He thus upbraids her, "and shod thee with violet-coloured shoes; and I girt thee about with fine linen, and clad thee with fine garments. I decked thee also with ornaments, and put bracelets on thy hands, and a chain about thy neck. And I put a jewel on thy forehead, and earrings in thine ears, and a beautiful crown upon thy head. . . . Thou wast perfect, through My Beauty which I put upon thee, saith the Lord, thy God."[1]

Then is the whole earth encompassed as with a snare; all the goodly arts of life wear a false aspect; and every darling joy wherewith the soul rejoices to surround its earthly dwelling-place becomes as a lure or a guile to deceive the children of men: their songs are as the songs of sirens; their cups brim over with enchantments to pervert the understanding. And to the perversion of the understanding, alas! is added the hereditary taint and malice of the heart: "The bewitching of vanity obscureth good things, and the wandering of concupiscence overturneth the innocent

---

[1] Ezech. xvi. 10-12, 14.

mind."[1] "For I am delighted with the Law of God," writes the Apostle, "according to the inward man; but I see another law in my members, fighting against the law of my mind, and captivating me in the law of sin which is in my members. Unhappy man that I am, who shall deliver me from the body of this death!"[2] This is the aspect of life's trial which so often prompts the cry, "Woe is me, that my sojourning is prolonged!"[3] and "Who will give me wings like a dove, and I will fly and be at rest!"[4] *I shall be satisfied when Thy Glory shall appear.*

Thus sin, or the disorder of nature induced by sin, is the account of illusion in the beautiful creations of God. And yet, even if we could regard them with the pure eyes of saints and angels, still, I repeat, we can rest in none of these things; for they do not rest in themselves: they point ever onward and upward unto God, and His "Glory that shall be revealed in us." He Himself has bound up with their very nature a rebuke for us, if ever we would abide in them as our sovereign repose and beatitude; or what else is the meaning of that which is so often complained, that pleasure palls and cloys, oftentimes even when it be innocent; that we live always in the past or the future, rather than in the present; that our sweetest songs are those of melancholy burden; that our most exalted delights have a savour that is near akin to pain; and that excess, alike of joy as grief, expresses itself in tears—as if

---

[1] Wisd. iv. 12. [2] Rom. vii. 22.
[3] Ps. cxix. 5. [4] Ps. liv. 7.

it were not quite natural in us to be happy? No: for since all beautiful and desirable objects in creation were only designed to raise our minds to the contemplation of the Sovereign Beauty, it would frustrate the very purpose of their appointment, if themselves were equal to appease the longing desire which they provoke: *I shall be satisfied when Thy Glory shall appear.*

My brethren, the Glory that shall be revealed hereafter, which at last will satisfy the earnest longing of our hearts, is inconceivable — unutterable. "Eye hath not seen, nor ear heard, nor hath it entered into the heart of man *to conceive* what things God hath prepared for them that love Him;"[1] yet thus much, at least, appears from what I have said (and it is enough for us), that to lose or gain the Sovereign Good is, in the very fact, to lose or gain everything which, in our heart of hearts, we had really loved and prized in this world. For the desire of God is natural to the heart of man: in this sense we cannot help but love Him. He is the end of our being; and, as such, though our will be against Him, and our footsteps far away from His paths, even yet does our whole nature blindly crave after Him, and our very love of creatures is a crooked love of God. Oh, then, what shall be the surprise and confusion of the sinner when he stands up to render account before the "great white Throne, and One sitting upon it from whose Face earth and heaven flee away, and there is no place found for them!"[2] Unhappy

---

[1] 1 Cor. ii. 9.   [2] Apoc. xx. 11.

man, who had vainly conceived that in his sinning he had only risked the forfeiture of certain vague, spiritual delights (for such he had accounted them) when he sees revealed, in the sacred Person of his Judge, as the soul is revealed in a face (for thus revealed, a brief moment, he shall see it), the sweet, awful Beauty of God! Then, in the words of the prophet Isaias, "the Light of Israel shall be as a Fire, and the Holy One thereof as a Flame"[1] to burn his heart with the memory of some sinless joy of happy childhood, or some noble art which he had cultivated in riper years, too subtle and refined, of its very nature, to be defiled like the rest, or some pure and tender object of affection which, abandoned as he was, had been the only sunny spot in a ruined life!

But O, the joyful surprise of the just: for shall not their joy be to them a surprise? They would seem, in the words of our Blessed Saviour, to have "hated their life" when upon earth; but they have loved it well indeed, since, in hating, they have "kept it unto life eternal." They had deemed it a point of wisdom to sacrifice this present world to the world to come; but O, felicitous prudence! since they are found in the event to have gained the substance both of one and the other, while they recover, in God, everything which they seemed to have lost in this world for His sweet love's sake.

"Come, ye blessed of My Father, possess you the kingdom which was prepared for you from the

[1] Isa. x. 17.

foundation of the world."[1] O happy welcome! O bright Day of Eternity! O blessed Mansion of the Heavenly City, in which Christ reigns for ever, together with His just made perfect, encompassed by the ministry of Angels, and worshipped by "a great multitude that no man could number, of all nations, and tribes, and peoples, and tongues,"[2] with hymns and canticles, in harmonies unutterable: where is love and bliss and peace and rest, secure, unalterable, evermore; and over all, O the unspeakable Face of God! which at last shall satisfy the weary, aching heart of man. O Splendid Truth, and Good, and Fair, and Holy! O Love! can I then nothing shape, or dream, or utter, to tell the Glory which Thou art? Ah, brethren, God were not God if thought could reach, or tongue could speak the wonder of that Blessed Vision which is our priceless hope as Sons of God; but "we know that when He shall appear we shall be like Him," and then "we shall see Him as He is."[3] He shall show us His Glory, unveiled; and, changed into His likeness, we shall bear to see It: we shall behold the very Face of God! This Vision is indeed unspeakable; and yet, surely, not quite as a Stranger, brethren, shall we welcome It. For God (it shall then be plainly manifest), God was what we had always loved and wanted; but, although we had "felt our hearts burning within us" what time He showed us His tokens, yet we knew not even why they burned; for our "eyes were

---

[1] Matt. xxv. 34.   [2] Apoc. vii. 9.
[3] 1 John iii. 2.

held" by vanity, and we had failed to recognise or them or Him. But now we know why it seemed there overhung earth's fairest shows, as if a halo not of earth; now we learn what it was music, with its mysterious voices, was striving to utter to our spirit; now we see that what so drew us to our earthly friends was His Light upon their faces: and sky and stars and sea and hill and flood, and all things beauteous and lovable, are revealed as a parable of the Glory of God and the riches of His imperishable Kingdom; and we shall *be satisfied because His Glory hath appeared.*

XVII.

THE VISIBLE AND SACRAMENTAL ADVENT.

"He shall abide with you and be in you: I will not leave you orphans; I will come to you."—JOHN xiv. 17, 18.

A SAD and mournful surprise indeed to the disciples was the announcement of their divine Master that He was about to leave them and to quit this world. So soon as they had really believed in their hearts that Jesus was the promised Saviour, they must have felt their privilege and their joy in it as something quite unutterable. Theirs, then, was the great Day of the Lord which so many kings and priests and prophets had tearfully desired, but which never, on this side of the grave, had their eyes been blessed with seeing. The Fathers of Old had lived under the cloud of God's wrath on a sinful world. In the latter days, it was written that One would come Who should make their peace, and God would reign with His people; but He only *was to come*, and they must sanctify themselves in that hope. "O that Thou wouldst rend the heavens and wouldst come down," exclaims Isaias; "the mountains would melt away at Thy Presence: they would melt as at the burning of fire, the waters would burn with fire, that Thy Name might be made known to Thine enemies; that the nations might tremble at Thy Presence. . . . From the beginning of the world they have not heard nor perceived with the ears: the eye hath not seen, O God, besides Thee, what things Thou hast prepared for them that wait for Thee."[1] Meanwhile the absence of God was as a desolation, and His silence ominous and oppressive. It is true that they had, to their great comfort, a deep and abiding sense of His *unseen* Presence in the world. They would read, instinctively, His "testimonies" in the great Book of Nature, which lay ever unrolled before their eyes; in the intimations of the heart and conscience; in the marvellous ordering of their singular history, with its stupendous miracles; and in so many special providences in their regard. But it was this very keenness of their spiritual apprehension of God which only intensified the feeling that He was, in the world of sense at least, "a hidden God," Who did not show Himself, nor did He speak. "But if I go to the East," says Holy Job, "He appeareth not; if to the West, I shall not understand Him; if to the left hand, what shall I do? I shall not lay hold on Him; if I turn myself to the right hand, I shall not see Him."[2] "O Expectation of Israel!" exclaims Jeremias, "why wilt Thou be as a stranger in the land, and as a way-

[1] Isa. lxiv. 1. [2] Job xxiii. 8.

faring man that turneth in to lodge? . . . But Thou, O Lord, art amongst us, and Thy Name is called upon us; forsake us not."[1] And in a similar strain complains the Psalmist: "Why, O Lord, hast Thou retired afar off? why dost Thou slight us in our wants, in the day of trouble?"[2] "Hold not Thy peace, neither be Thou still, O God: for lo! Thine enemies have made a noise, and they that hate Thee have lifted up the head;"[3] and, "O my God, be not Thou silent to me; lest, if Thou be silent to me, I become like them that go down into the pit."[4] Hence that craving after sensible signs and tokens, which, until the latter days, was a distinctive characteristic of the once chosen people of God; and which, in another shape, as it is expressed in a prayer of the royal Prophet, is not perhaps quite unknown amongst ourselves: "O, look upon me, and have mercy on me! . . . Show me *a token for good*, that they who hate me may see and be confounded; because Thou, O Lord, hast helped me and hast comforted me."[5]

But now, the Object Himself of all this ancient yearning, and loving complaint, had made an end at once of His absence and His silence; and that was fulfilled which the Psalmist had foretold: "God shall come *manifestly:* our God shall come, and shall not *keep silence;*"[6] and there was to be an end, if not altogether of signs and tokens, yet of all such signs and tokens as should stand in the stead of Himself;

---

[1] Jer. xiv. 8.   [2] Ps. x. 1.   [3] Ibid. lxxxii. 1.
[4] Ps. xxvii. 1.   [5] Ibid. lxxxv. 16.   [6] Ibid. xlix. 3.

for, "The Lord" Himself "shall be named as an everlasting Sign, which shall not be taken away."[1]

And He had come! O joy, O great, unspeakable Day of the Lord! The blind see; the lame walk; the deaf hear; the dumb speak; the lepers are cleansed; the dead are raised to life. Virtue went out from Him: there was healing in the very fringe of His garment. He spoke as one having authority: the winds and the seas obeyed Him; the very devils cried out and confessed Him; the Heavenly Father also Himself bare testimony of Him, in voices and signs from above. And yet, not for signs and wonders alone, such as these, did men believe (there were those who believed not for all the miracles that He wrought, but, out of their pride and hardness of heart, explained away, or accounted them to Beelzebub); but oh, it was Himself was the sweet, awful Sign, which gave to all His wondrous works conviction irresistible, and drew after Him, perforce, the hearts of men of faith and good-will! The sacred spell of His divine Presence, which St. John calls His Glory—"And we saw His glory, the glory, as it were, of the Only-begotten of the Father, full of grace and truth"[2]—the outward splendour of His hidden Majesty, which invested Him as with a halo of light,—this it was that so wrought on the Baptist, yet unborn; that he leaped in the womb for joy; and on holy Simeon, when he took the infant Saviour into his aged arms, and craved only the Lord's bidding to depart, since his eyes had seen

[1] Isa. lv. 13.   [2] John i. 14.

the Salvation of Israel. The disciples gladly left their craft and nets at His call; Levi rose up at once from "the customs;" Zaccheus forsook his dishonest practices; Magdalen found it a Paradise to weep out her sins at His feet. Men followed Him into the wilderness, in crowds of thousands, to seek after Everlasting Life, and feast their souls on His heavenly discourse.

And now, just when it seemed they were beginning to know Him, who He was, and to feel that Heaven had nothing better to bestow, or earth to receive, than Himself; and when they had thought that the time was accomplished wherein He should "restore the Kingdom to Israel," He began, instead, to "signify what death He should die:" which word, when Simon Peter heard for the first time, he *rebuked* Him: "Lord, be it far from Thee, he had said;" "this shall not be unto Thee."[1] And again, when now His hour drew nigh, He spoke to them freely and plainly; that "If the grain of wheat fall into the ground and die, it bringeth forth much fruit;"[2] that "The Son of Man must be lifted up from the earth;"[3] that, in short, "I go to the Father."[4] Mournful words, I say, and strange in their ears as mournful! "We have heard from out of the Law," answered the crowd, "that Christ abideth for ever; and how sayest Thou that the Son of Man must be lifted up?"[5] And some such thought as this must have been at the root of the Apostles' sorrow, what time their beloved

---

[1] Matt. xvi. 22. [2] John xii. 24. [3] Ibid. xii. 32-34.
[4] Ibid. xvi. 10. [5] Ibid. xii. 34.

Master spoke to them, at the Last Supper, His farewell words, though their grief was dumb, and they gave it no utterance: "But because I have spoken these things to you," He said, "sorrow hath filled your heart."[1] Alas, indeed, and well they might be sorrowful! Were all their fresh-budding hopes to be dashed again to earth? Was the Sun to set on their hearts, or ever it grew unto the perfect day? Their new-found Glory, was it to be made void, even like the brightness on Moses' face which was its symbol? And must the darkness that was of old return, but more dismal, and the absence become drearier, and the silence more insufferable; because the Light had been, and it was dark; He had come, and He was gone; He had spoken, and they should hear His voice no more?

He did not strive to check their grief: it must have its course. Excess of sorrow, in a manner, works out its own relief; and theirs was a sorrow which, like that of a woman who "is in anguish because her hour is come," would shortly be changed into joy. And, if He told them that it was "expedient" for themselves that He should go; but that He would not leave them orphans; and spoke of the Comforter He would send them from the Father; yet He looked for the full fruit of His words, not now, when their minds were still dark and carnal, and their hearts overcharged with grief, but hereafter: "I have yet many things to say to you," He said, "but you cannot bear them now."[2] He would

[1] John xvi. 6.   [2] Ibid. xvi. 12.

seem, from the very nature of the case, to "speak to them in proverbs;" for the mind, like the eye, does not readily adjust itself to a new light; and the disciples had much to learn in a short space; and, what is a still more difficult matter, they had much to *unlearn*. They might marvel, if in their grief they considered His words attentively, that He should speak of "another Comforter," while He declared to them in the same breath, as it were, that He was *coming back Himself:* "He shall abide with you, and be in you: I will not leave you orphans; *I* will come to you;" and still more might they marvel that His very going was to be the means of His coming: "You have heard that I said to you, 'I go away, and I come unto you.'"[1] But He sought not now to explain to them the meaning of His words,— which He planted in their hearts to grow and ripen unto fruit in due season. What He had before signified to Peter of His acts, that, "What I do you know not now, but you shall know hereafter,"[2] this He now declared to them also of His divine words: "But the Paraclete, the Holy Ghost, Whom the Father will send in My Name, He will teach you all things, and bring all things to your mind, whatsoever I shall have said to you."[3] The Holy Spirit would in due time reveal to them, in its fulness, the comfort which was in store for them, which, after all, would be best known in the experience.

But howsoever obscure His words might appear, until the event should unfold their meaning, the

[1] John xiv. 28.   [2] Ibid. xiii. 7.   [3] Ibid. xiv. 26.

THE VISIBLE AND SACRAMENTAL ADVENT.

promise itself was distinct and definite,—that, as surely as He was now going away, so surely also would He come back. He did not merely promise the disciples that the Comforter should supply His place (alas, they would only think, what Comforter could be better than Himself?) but that the Holy Spirit should *bring back Himself*. "He shall abide with you, and be in you;" (once more) "I will not leave you orphans; *I* will come to you." *He*, the "Word made Flesh," God and Man in one Person, Whose Face they saw, and Who conversed with them, Who was about to leave them—but He would come back, He said; He would return to them in His Spirit, but none the less truly, on that account, would He also return to them in Himself, though the Holy Spirit was to be the Medium of His return. As He had come, was conceived, made flesh, and born into this world, by virtue of the Holy Ghost, even so, by virtue of the same Holy Spirit would He return therein.

But when, and in what manner would He return? since this is a question which as narrowly and dearly concerns ourselves, as those to whom the promise was given. We know that He will come again in the Last Day, when He will judge all mankind, and deliver up His Kingdom into the hands of His Father; but it is clear, from His own divine words, that not this, His Second, and manifest Coming, was intended by them, but an immediate Advent, consequent upon, and to be obtained through, His very departure; so that He was *really*, if not *manifestly*, to abide for ever, as it had been foretold of Him. Neither did He mean that He would return to them in His Resurrection from the dead; though this also was promised: "But I will see you again, and your heart shall rejoice; and your joy no man shall take from you:"[1] for, after He was arisen as He had said, still He spoke *of going;* and still, if we consider well the mystery of His divine words, He spoke also of coming back: "Touch Me not;" He said to Magdalen, at the Sepulchre, "for I am not yet ascended to my Father."[2] If, therefore, she must not touch Him *now*, because He was not ascended, it is clear that she *should* touch Him *when He was ascended* (howsoever that was to be). And what He had thus insinuated to Mary Magdalen, of a mysterious contact, and communion with Him, when she should no longer see His Face upon earth, this He also vouchsafed to *act* before the very eyes of the disciples, at Emmaus, with every circumstance of impressive significance. For, although they had "felt their hearts burning within them," as He discoursed with them by the way, yet "their eyes were held that they should not know Him," until He supped with them at the inn; when "He took bread, and blest, and gave to them, and their eyes were opened, and they knew Him; and He vanished out of their sight"[3]—leaving behind Him the sacramental Token! For think not, brethren, that what is here styled the "breaking of bread" was nothing more than an ordinary supper, since it was attended by an action

[1] John xvi. 22. [2] Ibid. xx. 17. [3] Luke xxiv. 30.

so significant as to open the eyes of these disciples to discern the Lord and Saviour beneath the disguise of their pilgrim guest. "They knew Him," we read, "in the breaking of bread;"[1] but how should they have known Him therein, unless indeed it were that solemn breaking of bread, which He appointed at His Last Supper, whereof the Apostle testifies where He says: "The Chalice of benediction which we bless, is it not the communion of the Blood of Christ? And the Bread which we break, is it not the partaking of the Body of the Lord?"[2] Can one longer doubt in what manner He should come back, and Magdalen and the disciples should "touch and handle of the Word of Life," after He was ascended to the Father?

By such gracious intimations as these, and others doubtless that are unrecorded, did our Blessed Saviour school the minds of the disciples to regard His departure from this world as the signal of an Advent far more blessed and intimate than was even His visible presence in the flesh; and with such goodly result, that instead of the "sad discourses" which they had held with one another on His death, it was with hearts of praise and thanksgiving that they beheld Him ascend into Heaven: "They adored," we read, "and went back into Jerusalem with great joy; and they were always in the temple praising and blessing God."[3] And then, when the days of Pentecost were accomplished, the Holy Ghost came down upon them, and completed the

[1] Luke xxiv. 35. [2] 1 Cor. x. 16. [3] Luke xxiv. 52.

lesson by bringing the Glory of the Face of Jesus into their hearts. "For God, Who commanded the light to shine out of darkness," says the Apostle, "hath *shined in our hearts*, to give the light of the knowledge of the glory of God, in the Face of Christ Jesus."[1] They had lost—that they might the better find Him.

And thus, brethren, was the disciples' sorrow changed into the gladness which is also our portion; for we have not, like them, lost our Lord, and we have found Him; and without the experience of their grief we have entered into all their joy. O what words can we find suitable wherein to express the fulness of our blessedness, if only we have known the day of our visitation. The Fathers of Old deplored the absence of God from the world of His creation; and desired with longing hearts that the Prince of Peace should come; they grieved for His silence; they craved after signs and tokens: He is come, and He "abideth for ever" in the Sacrament of His Love; He has spoken, and His words still live in our heart for a lamp to our footsteps; nor (for signs are for unbelievers, and tokens for them that are sundered) do we desire another sign or token than Himself. The disciples beheld the Face of Jesus in the Flesh: it was an inestimable privilege; and yet, surely, they hardly knew Him, until they knew, as we also know Him, "in the breaking of bread;" when He vanished from their sight, that He might enter into their hearts; that,

[1] 2 Cor. iv. 6.

He abiding in them, and they in Him, in the uttermost consummation of love and union, they could taste and see indeed that the Lord is sweet. They anxiously expected the manifestation of His Glory, when He should come into His Kingdom; nor did they first taste until, as He had promised, they had seen the Kingdom of God coming in power: but, behold, instead of the regal splendour of David's house, a Kingdom worthy of David's Son Whom David himself, in the spirit, called Lord—the Kingdom of Heaven upon earth! For such in truth, to the eyes of faith, is the Church of God, wherein is the desirable Presence of Jesus enthroned in His earthly Sanctuary; and such it is described in the words of the Apostle: "For you are not come," he says, "to a mountain that might be touched, and a burning fire, and a whirlwind, and darkness, and storm, and the sound of a trumpet, and the voice of words, . . . but you are come to Mount Sion, and to the City of the Living God, the Heavenly Jerusalem, and to the company of many thousands of angels, and to the Church of the first-born, who are written in the heavens, and to God, the Judge of all, and to the spirits of the just made perfect, and to Jesus, the Mediator of the New Testament, and to the sprinkling of Blood that speaketh better than Abel."[1] Already, and in this our day are fulfilled the words which St. John heard, in his vision of the Holy City coming down from Heaven: "Behold the Tabernacle of God with men; and He will dwell

[1] Heb. xii. 18, 22.

with them; and they shall be His people; and God with them shall be their God."[1] For, in the Sacramental Advent is vouchsafed us, not so much a type of Heaven, as rather an earnest and foretaste which, hereafter, shall pass into, and be absorbed in it; when the veil shall be uplifted, and we shall see, face to face, Him Whom now we faithfully adore; Who already wipes away the tears from our eyes, quickens our mortal bodies unto everlasting Life, and feasts our souls with the plenitude of His House. What more in this world, brethren, can we ask or desire? "For what have I in Heaven, and besides Thee, what do I desire upon earth ... the God of my heart, and the God that is my portion for ever?"[2] "How lovely are Thy tabernacles, O Lord of Hosts: my soul longeth and fainteth for the courts of the Lord; my heart and my flesh have exulted in God, my Saviour. For the sparrow hath found herself a house, and the turtle a nest for herself where she may lay her young ones: Thine altars, O Lord of Hosts, my King, and my God! Blessed are they who dwell in Thy House; they shall praise Thee for ever and ever!"[3]

[1] Apoc. xxi. 3. [2] Ps. lxxii. 25, 26. [3] Ibid. lxxxiii. 1.

XVIII.

THE GIFT OF THE HOLY SPIRIT.

"Ascending on High, He led captivity captive; He gave gifts to men."—EPH. iv. 8.

THE Heavenly Father has given to us many most precious gifts, both in the order of nature and in the order of grace; but in the season of Pentecost we are called upon to commemorate, while we adore with hearts of praise and thanksgiving, that Holy Spirit of God, Who is Himself, not merely, as the Hymn says, "best Gift of God to man," but also, as it will appear, the necessary channel and medium by which "every best and perfect gift coming down from the Father of Lights"[1] is bestowed upon us; as it is written of our Blessed Saviour in the text that, "Ascending on High, He led captivity captive: He gave gifts to men." For thus He had promised, when about to leave the world: "I will ask the Father," He had said, "and He shall give you another Paraclete or

[1] James i. 17.

Comforter, that He may abide with you for ever; the Spirit of Truth, Whom the world cannot receive, because it seeth Him not, nor knoweth Him; but you shall know Him, because He shall abide with you and be in you;"[1] and in this Gift, I say, all other gifts were included.

Now I propose to inquire, together with you, brethren, on this solemn festival, as to what is the nature of this Promise, now accomplished in us, of the Gift of the Holy Spirit. Something unspeakably great and overwhelming (far more so than we can ever fully comprehend) it must be, to justify the exalted terms in which St. Peter speaks of it, for instance, when he says that God hath given us, "through Jesus Christ, our Lord, most great and precious promises, that by these you may be made *partakers of the divine nature;* flying the corruption of that concupiscence which is in the world."[2] I would ask, in all humility (so far as it is given us to know it), what is that Gift, so pre-eminently best, that even the Face of God, in Christ, must be withdrawn from earth to make room for it; since He said to His disciples: "It is expedient for you that I go; for, if I go not, the Paraclete will not come to you: but, if I go, I will send Him to you:"[3] while again the same precious Gift gives Christ back again to us; for He returns to us in His Spirit: "He shall abide with you and be in you: I will not leave you orphans; I will come to you."[4] And as we owe certain special

---

[1] John xiv. 16, 17. [2] 2 Peter i. 4.
[3] John xvi. 7. [4] Ibid. xiv. 17, 18.

regards of gratitude and affection to each of the divine Persons, as distinct Persons, I would learn in what especial manner we are indebted to the Holy Spirit, that we should be attracted to Him with a love and devotion proper to Himself? But to this end it will be necessary to consider the several divine Persons in their respective relations, One towards Another; and it will be the natural course to consider, in the first place, the Gift, as in Itself; and, secondly, the manner of Its communication.

I. The Three divine Persons of the Holy Trinity, the Father, the Son, and the Holy Ghost, while they are quite distinct as Persons, are, as our holy Faith teaches, simply One Indivisible God. Moreover, they are inseparable; as in their common divine Nature, so in their works. The Father is not the Author of one creation, the Son of another, and the Holy Ghost of a third; but, in each and all of the works of God, one undivided operation and efficiency must be confessed of the whole Trinity. Thus, in the creation of man, it was said: " Let us make man to our own image and likeness;"[1] wherein the plurality of divine Persons is insinuated, as combined in operation. Again, in the great work of man's Redemption, the Three several Persons are exhibited as concurring—the Father, "Who so loved the world as to give His Only-begotten Son, that whosoever believeth in Him may not perish,"[2] the Son Himself, Who was "obedient unto death,"[3] and the Holy Spirit, by Whose overshadowing

[1] Gen. i. 26.   [2] John iii. 16.   [3] Phil. ii. 8.

virtue the mystery of the Incarnation was accomplished; although it was the divine Son only, and not the Father or the Holy Ghost, Who was made man, and died for us upon the Cross.

Still, this union of operation does not forbid, what is indeed distinctly asserted in Holy Scripture, that each of the several divine Persons has His own proper office, and the special ministrations (if one may worthily speak so) pertaining to it. For although the Three Persons agree in power, and wisdom, and sanctity, and other essential attributes of the Godhead, yet this order (not indeed of time, but of origin and dependency) obtains amongst them —viz., that the Father is, in the nature of the case, the Origin, and, as it were, the Fountain of the whole Trinity; for the Son is "begotten of the Father;" while the Holy Ghost "proceeds" from the Father and the Son. But the same order is also assigned, in Holy Scripture, to the efficiency of the Three divine Persons in the works of God; since it declares that God the Father, *through* the divine Son, and *in* the Holy Ghost, created all things. Thus, "There is but one God," writes St. Paul, "the Father, *of* Whom are all things, . . . and one Lord, Jesus Christ, *by* Whom are all things," . . . "and" (as another version adds) "one Holy Ghost, *in* Whom are all things."[1] And again, having respect to the same order, "For *of* Him, and *by* Him, and *in* Him are all things: to Him be glory for ever. Amen."[2]

In accordance, therefore, with this sacred Hierarchy

---

[1] 1 Cor. viii. 6. [2] Rom. xi. 36.

in the Holy Trinity, we may chiefly consider in the Father the Almighty Power and sovereign Fecundity of God, Who created the heavens and the earth, with "all the furniture" and adornment thereof, out of nothing by His only Word; "in Whom we live and move and be;"[1] Who is the awful Founder and Upholder of all reality. We shall rightly also ascribe to the divine Son, considered as the "Word" or Wisdom of the Father, whatsoever the mind discerns in this visible creation of art or design, of skill or method, fitness and symmetry, of concord, harmony, regularity, and beauty. And so, likewise (to come to the subject which has to be treated on this high Festival), do we regard the Holy Spirit as the Giver of life, and light, and strength to all created things. He it was Who, in the beginning, brooded like a dove over the uninformed and formless chaos, infusing the vital genial heat into the first blind, incipient, rudimental forces, or seeds of things; stirring and upheaving the discordant elements in the dark womb of earth; making light out of darkness; bringing the lawless under rule; and thus co-operating with the divine Word to shed the smile of beauty and glory over the works of God. His office and work, as in creation, so is in renewal; as it is written: "Thou shalt send forth Thy Spirit, and they shall be created: and Thou shalt renew the face of the earth;"[2] as indeed we see the face of the earth to be renewed in this Spring-time of the year; when universal nature, which had seemed heretofore as in

---

[1] Acts xvii. 28. [2] Ps. ciii. 30.

a state of death, or death-like sleep, suddenly stirs, breathes, awakes, and is recruited through her whole frame; and every herb, and shrub, and tree bursts out into exuberant life; and man and beast are gladdened and refreshed; and flowers unbosom their loveliness, and perfume the air with their fragrance; and the bird pants out its heart in raptures of inextinguishable song. These are Thy works, most high and most deep, most sweet and comforting Spirit, proceeding of the love of the Father and the Son. And if, my brethren, we cannot rightly know Him as He is, in the sovereign rest and beatitude of His Eternity, or search into the unspeakable mystery of His divine Personality, at least we can contemplate Him, in effect, in these fair and goodly fruits of His earthly ministrations; not indeed as forgetting for a moment those unspeakably higher blessings which He has prepared for us in the order of grace, but as thankful to God for all His mercies, and for every gift, each good and best in its own kind; and as evincing our gratitude in the very remembrance of them.

Such, then, is the Holy Ghost, as He is graciously revealed from without in the works of creation; as the Breath of God or Spirit of Life to universal nature. And what He manifests Himself without, that also is He within the soul of man; being the Source as well of the natural life by which he lives, as of the supernatural, or divine Life, whereby He lives to God. Not, again, as if the Father were not Himself the Author of life; for to Him are referred the words, "In Him we live and move and be;" nor that the divine Son is not also Himself "a Quickening Spirit,"[1] as the Apostle actually styles Him; but according to the order which I have just now stated, whereby God the Father, through the Son and in the Holy Ghost, creates, ordains, and quickens all things. This is the account of the prominence which is assigned in Holy Scripture to the operations of the Holy Spirit, that His action is more immediate; because while the Father and the Son equally operate, yet they only operate in Him. Hence He is called the "Finger of God,"[2] as being the essential Medium whereby God is brought into contact with His creatures; the Instrument of divine power wherewith He ever acts in nature or in grace. Thus it was of the Holy Spirit that the Ancient Fathers understood what is written concerning the creation of the First Adam; how that the Lord God, when He had fashioned him a body "of the slime of the earth," "breathed into his face the Breath of Life, and man became a living soul."[3] It was by virtue of the same Holy Spirit that Christ, the Second Adam, was conceived, "made flesh," and born into this world.[4] And what we read of His sacred life is in accordance with His miraculous Advent. He acts of Himself; but He acts *in* the Holy Ghost. He was "led by the Spirit into the desert;"[5] He "returned, in the power of the Spirit, into Galilee;"[6]

---

[1] 1 Cor. xv. 45.
[2] Luke xi.; Matt. xii. 28.
[3] Gen. ii. 7.
[4] Matt. i. 20; John i. 13, 14.
[5] Matt. iv. 1.
[6] Luke iv. 14.

He "cast out devils" by "the Spirit of God;"[1] He "rejoiced in the Holy Ghost;"[2] and (what is even more striking) it was in the power of the Holy Spirit that He was raised up from the dead, and that we also must be raised up in His Likeness; as the Apostle testifies where he says that: "If the Spirit of Him Who raised up Jesus Christ from the dead dwell in you, He that raised up Jesus Christ from the dead shall also quicken *your* mortal bodies, *because of His Spirit that dwelleth in you.*"[3]

And lastly, as the Hymn reminds us, the Holy Spirit is that "Unction from the Holy One"[4] which constitutes the virtue and efficiency of sacraments, wherein the "weak and needy elements" of the older Covenant yield to ordinances instinct with divine Life; and the baptism of water is "in the Holy Ghost and in Fire;" the anointing of oil imparts the strength of God; the homely symbols of bread and wine communicate the Word Incarnate; and invested with the Priesthood of Jesus Christ, a son of man absolves the sins of men.

Such considerations as these are not only to the purpose, as declaring to us the quality of the heavenly Gift which was bestowed on us in the day of Pentecost; but they go still further, and suggest to us why He is emphatically the "Gift of God," in a distinct sense, in which the Father or the Son, from the very nature of the case, is not, and so furnish us with the motive of a devotion which shall be,

---

[1] Matt. xii. 28. [2] Luke x. 21. [3] Rom. viii. 11.
[4] 1. John ii. 20.

as I said, proper and peculiar to Himself. For if all the divine works, whether of the Father or the Son, are only wrought by the co-operation of the Holy Ghost; if He is thus God's Quickening Breath, the Finger of His Power and Spiritual Unction, then it is manifest that this Holy Spirit, Who is Himself the ineffable Bond of Love between the Father and the Son, is also the very Link whereby God is brought into communion with His creatures. It is thus the special note or property of His divine Person that He is the Gift, communicated indeed in the fulness of time, but everlastingly communicable, in Whom, through Christ, "we have *access* both in one Spirit to the Father," and "are built together into an habitation of God."[1]

But, as in the works of Creation and Redemption, so in our Sanctification the whole Trinity is concerned, although our Sanctification is wrought immediately by the Holy Spirit, as our Redemption by God the Son. For the Holy Ghost abides in us of Himself, the Father, and the Son in Him. "He shall abide with you, and be in you," our Blessed Saviour has said; "I will not leave you orphans; I will come to you."[2] And whereas He had before said to Philip, "Believe you not that I am in the Father, and the Father in Me?"[3] we see, putting the two texts together, that God the Father, through the Son, abides in the hearts of those who are in grace in His Holy Spirit; according to the comforting assurance of our Blessed Saviour that, "If any man love

---

[1] Eph. ii. 18, 22. [2] John xiv. 17, 18. [3] Ibid. v. 11.

Me he will keep My Word, and My Father will love him, and we will come unto him, and make our abode with him."[1]

2. And thus I am led to speak of the manner in which the heavenly Gift is communicated to us. And here, though I would not willingly appear to be over subtle, yet, at the same time, we ought to understand very distinctly the nature of our awful privilege. The Holy Spirit, forasmuch as He is God, is everywhere, and in all things: and hence it might be imagined that He therefore indwells in all things, only with this difference, that He indwells in the souls of the just in a more solemn manner. Now I say that God is *in* all things, if you will, but He is not therefore *within* all things. He could not, for instance, be said, with any intelligible 'meaning, to indwell in material objects; and for the simple reason that mere matter has no capacity. For so often as you divide its surface another surface is revealed: it has in reality *no inside*. On the other hand, it is in a very real sense that a man says, speaking of one time, that there was *a void* within his breast, and, of another, that his heart was *very full;* because the heart of man, as the vessel of an immortal spirit, has that very capacity which in matter is essentially wanting. But even where the capacity exists, God only indwells in His creatures in the measure of His own goodwill and loving condescension; and by no constraint of His nature, seeing that His Substance is clearer than the light,

[1] John xiv. 23.

and more subtle than thought, and so, as the language of Holy Scripture implies, admits of every kind and degree of communication, between the plenitude of "peace which passeth understanding," and the darksome horror of absolute estrangement.

Thus the ancient Patriarchs and Prophets of old proclaimed to the world that the Spirit of God was with their spirit; and so in one sense He was. He did not indeed *indwell*, but He *inwrought* in them, and enriched their souls with spiritual influences. It was the visitations of His grace which were to them as if the Face of God; whence Holy David exclaims: "Cast me not away from Thy Face, and take not Thy Holy Spirit from me."[1] This was their gift in their day, to be enlightened, healed, and strengthened, and comforted by the operations of the Holy Spirit within their hearts: but what is ours? I have already said it; but O, my brethren, can we ever understand it, or even find suitable words wherein to express the utter blessedness of it? No longer, as it were, the mere fragrance of the heavenly Unction, but the precious Nard, Itself in Substance, is poured into our vessels, if so be only that we are in the grace of God. "In this we know," says St. John, "that we abide in Him, and He in us, because He hath given us of His Spirit."[2] And again: "You shall know Him, because He shall abide with you, and be in you."[3] And that this is no mere phrase, metaphor, or allowable exaggeration, but doctrine, or statement of fact, is sufficiently indicated by a

[1] Ps. l. 12.   [2] 1 John iv. 13.   [3] John xiv. 17.

consequence which is drawn from it, and which deserves our most serious attention—viz., that, through His indwelling in our souls, our bodies are made temples of the Holy Ghost. "For you are temples of the Living God," says St. Paul; "as God saith: 'I will dwell in them, and walk in them; and they shall be My people.'"[1] And again: "Know you not that your members are the Temple of the Holy Ghost, who is in you, whom you have from God. . . . Glorify, and bear God in your body."[2] And lastly, in words of awful warning: "But if any man violate the Temple of God, Him shall God destroy. For the Temple of God is holy, which you are."[3]

Contemplate, my brethren, this Gift of the Holy Spirit, which is in your souls, in your mortal bodies. What does He there? What is His office, and work, and what the kind and manner of His visitation? He pleads for you before the Father, or rather He pleads in you; as it is written: "For we know not what we should pray for as we ought; but the Spirit Himself asketh for us with unspeakable groanings."[4] He "helpeth our infirmity;" He strives with the corruption in us, whether it be sin, or the manifold misery of nature which is the result and consequence of sin; He enlightens the understanding; He strengthens the will to good; He tempers and orders in us the several affections and passions, and thus restores, in a measure, that just balance of the soul's powers, which the sin of Adam had

---

[1] 2 Cor. vi. 16.   [2] 1 Cor. vi. 19, 20.   [3] 1 Cor. iii. 17.
[4] Rom. viii. 26.

overthrown, wherein consists true liberty, when the reason is obedient to God, and the passions in subjection to the reason. He counsels; He guides; He comforts; He shows us the Face of God; He seals us in the image of Jesus Christ. He wholly quickens and informs us, body and soul, unto everlasting Life: whence we are no longer "in the flesh, but in the Spirit," "a new creature," "sons of God, and joint-heirs with Christ"[1] in His heavenly Kingdom. O, how difficult it is to realise what we are, and what we are capable of becoming, through this sublime and unspeakable Gift of the Spirit! "Behold, what manner of charity the Father hath bestowed upon us," says St. John, "that we should be, and should be called the sons of God! Therefore the world knoweth us not, because it knew not Him. Dearly beloved, we are now the sons of God, and it hath not yet appeared what we shall be. We know that, when He shall appear, we shall be like Him, because we shall see Him as He is. And every one that hath this hope in him sanctifieth himself, as He also is holy."[2] And thus the beloved disciple reminds us, that the Holy Ghost is not only a present blessing, but a pledge and earnest of still higher and better things which can never be fulfilled in us in this life.

And here I cannot forbear to indulge the expression of one sad thought that obtrudes itself, which is this; that we are hardly emboldened to look forward to that higher blessedness which, we trust, the Holy Spirit has in store for us, when we reflect

[1] Rom. viii. 17. [2] 1 John iii. 1, *et seq.*

how poorly even the best of us avail ourselves of this present benefit, which is at our disposal. The work of the Holy Ghost is hindered in us; and you know, my brethren, what hinders it. It is our poor appreciation of the Gift, and our faulty, feeble co-operation with Him. Hence it is, that, although we trust that we are in grace, we are not so happy, oftentimes, as we might be, and as we ought to be. We want that solid peace and calm joy which overflows on the very faces of holy men. Alas, it is the thought of our manifold sins and defects which often clouds to us the Face of God! The fact, also, that we are sometimes so sensitive to the many miseries which beset us, which are not our fault, but only our trial, shows how imperfectly the work of the Holy Spirit is accomplished in us. The Kingdom of God is within us, and we have not known it. He is lavish towards us of the riches and abundance of His House, and we have not yet learnt how to prize or turn them to account, as we ought. And, if this be the case with us, what other remedy or better have we than to turn to this same gentle Guest, Whom we trust that we have, at least this day, received into our breast? Surely He will hear the cry of our heart for His light, His healing, and His peace: or rather, it is Himself that prompts the prayer, Who prays in us, and with us, and Who has already prevailed before the Father's Face! It is Himself by the token that the very tears He sometimes makes us shed over our own unworthiness, are still sweeter than all the pleasures of this world. These are His "unspeakable groanings" for the fulfilment in us of "the adoption of the sons of God, the redemption of our body."[1] God grant that His work be speedily accomplished in us. Amen.

[1] Rom. viii. 23.

THE END.

PRINTED BY BALLANTYNE, HANSON AND CO.
EDINBURGH AND LONDON.

www.ingramcontent.com/pod-product-compliance
Lightning Source LLC
Chambersburg PA
CBHW031354230426
43670CB00006B/536